"I highly recommend this workbook for those struggling with eating disorders, and for all clinicians in the field. This book provides new insights into the development and treatment of eating disorders, offering what will undoubtably be a missing piece for many. The reader is invited to explore emotional overcontrol; social signaling; the role of playfulness and connection; and feelings such as envy, bitterness, and shame. This is an exceptional contribution to the field and there is simply nothing like it available to our clients. Engaging, relatable, and refreshing, this is a book you are going to want to read and share!"

—**Anita Federici, PhD, CPsych, FAED**, owner of the Centre for Psychology and
  Emotion Regulation; and adjunct faculty at York University in Toronto, ON, Canada

"Therapy workbooks are seldom 'good reads,' usually only coming alive once they become part of treatment. However, this is a great deal more than a workbook, weaving together a range of perspectives that together provide an informative, insightful, and thought-provoking book. I strongly recommend the book to anyone wishing to gain new insights into how emotions and the way we handle them—both individually and in social situations—get tangled up in eating disorders."

—**Ivan Eisler, OBE, PhD**, emeritus professor at King's College London, and
  joint head of the Maudsley Centre for Child and Adolescent Eating Disorders

The Radically Open DBT Workbook *for* Eating Disorders

FROM OVERCONTROL & LONELINESS TO RECOVERY & CONNECTION

KARYN D. HALL, PhD
ELLEN ASTRACHAN-FLETCHER, PhD
MIMA SIMIC, MD

New Harbinger Publications, Inc.

Publisher's Note

NEW HARBINGER PUBLICATIONS is a registered trademark of New Harbinger Publications, Inc.

New Harbinger Publications is an employee-owned company.

Distributed in Canada by Raincoast Books

Cover design by Sara Christian
Acquired by Catharine Meyers
Edited by Jennifer Eastman

Library of Congress Cataloging-in-Publication Data

Names: Hall, Karyn D., author. | Astrachan-Fletcher, Ellen, author. | Simic, Mima (Psychiatrist), author.
Title: The radically open DBT workbook for eating disorders : from overcontrol and loneliness to recovery and connection / Karyn D. Hall, Ellen Astrachan-Fletcher and Mima Simic.
Description: Oakland : New Harbinger Publications, 2022. | Includes bibliographical references.
Identifiers: LCCN 2021058421 | ISBN 9781684038930 (trade paperback)
Subjects: LCSH: Eating disorders--Treatment. | Dialectical behavior therapy.
Classification: LCC RC552.E18 H34 2022 | DDC 616.85/26--dc23/eng/20211207
LC record available at https://lccn.loc.gov/2021058421

Printed in the United States of America

24   23   22

10   9   8   7   6   5   4   3   2

Contents

Foreword

When we feel part of a tribe—we feel safe.

—T. R. Lynch

Humans are a hyper-cooperative species—more so than any other animal species. We engage in highly complex and coordinated group activities with non-kin and comply without resistance to requests from complete strangers. Research shows that rather than falling apart or running amuck when disaster strikes, most humans are calm and orderly, and work together to help others. During times of extreme crisis, we forget about our individual differences, backgrounds, and beliefs and unite for a common cause. For example, ask anyone closely involved in the 9/11 crisis in New York City the extent they were worried about whether the person they were helping was homeless or a millionaire, religious or atheist, black or white.

A core component of this evolutionary advantage involved the development of complex social-signaling capabilities that allowed for a quick and safe means to evaluate and resolve conflict and to manage potential collaborations. Our social-signaling capacities are more powerful than most individuals realize, as they viscerally impact not only the person we are interacting with but also our *own* physiology—most often at the preconscious level. Slow-motion film analysis has robustly revealed that we react to changes in the body movement, posture, and facial expressions of others during interactions without ever knowing it. Indeed, we are constantly social-signaling when around others (e.g., micro-expressions, body movements)—even when deliberately trying not to. This means that silence can be just as powerful as nonstop talking.

For our very early ancestors living in harsh environments, the cost of not detecting a signal of disapproval was too high to ignore—since banishment from the tribe* was essentially a death sentence from

---

* The use of the word "tribe" in RO DBT is meant to foster an understanding of our evolutionary history—hunter-gatherer bands of people that were dependent on each other for survival. These small groups were more than families (they weren't all genetically related) but less than a city, state, or nation—these concepts were outside of humanity's experience at that time. This term is based on anthropological and evolutionary psychological perspectives where hunter-gather tribes are generally understood to have been egalitarian; everyone was equal in worth and status. Our goal is to help clients (and therapists) understand that, from a RO perspective, to be psychologically healthy, we are all evolutionarily hard-wired to need a sense of belonging to a small group of people who care about our well-being, and whom we care about.

starvation or predation. Consequently, we are constantly scanning the social signals of others for signs of disapproval and are biologically predisposed to read them as disapproving—especially when they're ambiguous. *This means we are essentially a socially anxious species.* Blank expressions, furrowed brows, or slight frowns are often interpreted as disapproving—regardless of the actual intentions of the sender (some people frown or furrow their brow when concentrating). Moreover, being rejected hurts—research shows that social ostracism triggers the same areas of the brain that are triggered when we experience physical pain. Thus, we fear the pain of exclusion, and our emotional well-being is highly dependent on the extent we feel socially connected.

When I first began to develop principles for helping individuals who experience overcontrolled coping, I was unaware of just how much the final intervention would emphasize the importance of social signaling as a primary mechanism of change (see radically open dialectical behavior therapy treatment manuals; Lynch 2018a and 2018b). Overcontrolled coping is characterized by a strong desire to control one's environment, restrained emotional expression, limited social interaction, problems with close relationships, and rigid and inflexible responses to change. And it became increasingly clear over time that the main downsides of overcontrolled coping (often called "maladaptive overcontrol") were primarily social in nature. These individuals tend to be serious about life, set high personal standards, work hard, behave appropriately, and frequently will sacrifice personal needs to achieve desired goals or help others; yet inwardly they often feel clueless about how to join in with others or establish intimate bonds. For example, overcontrolled individuals tend to perceive new or unfamiliar (especially social) situations as potentially dangerous, so they will tend to mask or inhibit expressions of emotion, which often damages close social bonds and leads to misunderstanding or distrust, because it is hard for others to read their true feelings or intentions. Often no one outside the immediate family is aware of an overcontrolled individual's inner psychological distress. Moreover, since self-control is highly valued by most societies, the problems associated with excessive inhibitory control have received little attention or have been misunderstood. Most treatments do not recognize maladaptive overcontrol as a problem, so most overcontrolled clients suffer in silence.

What is exciting to me is that this book represents an important means of addressing this gap by providing step-by-step guidance on how to address problems of overcontrol with a special emphasis on eating-disordered (ED) problems like anorexia nervosa. Radically open dialectical behavior therapy (RO DBT) differs from many other treatment modalities because it does not consider restricted or ritualized eating to be the primary problem. Instead, the focus is on social-signaling deficits interfering with social connectedness. Thus, the book you are about to read considers anorexia nervosa and related ED problems as *symptoms* or *consequences* of maladaptive overcontrol (OC) coping. Research shows that perfectionistic and overcontrolled styles of coping often *precede* the development of eating disorder symptomatology. Wow!

The good news is that the book you are reading is informed by an evidence-based treatment; the research literature supports the efficacy of RO DBT in the treatment of overcontrolled disorders, including patients with anorexia nervosa, autism, chronic depression, and overcontrolled personality disorders (see

Gilbert et al. 2020 for review). Secondly, this book has been inspired and written by three of our most senior RO DBT clinician scientists—Karyn Hall PhD, Ellen Astrachan-Fletcher PhD, and Mima Simic MD—all of whom I have had the good fortune to collaborate with and supervise over multiple years, and perhaps, more importantly, I consider each a good friend. They were all intensively trained by me years before publication of the RO DBT treatment manuals (Lynch 2018a, 2018b) and are founding members of the RO DBT Senior Clinician Team, which provides oversight and guidance on our ongoing dissemination efforts. I know from personal experience that each of them actively practices the RO skills you will read about in this book, and each has had years of experience teaching and supervising clinicians in RO DBT. Their collective experience made it possible for them to creatively transform core RO DBT principles into a practical self-help guide that can be used either on its own or as a means of supplementing professional therapy.

What is also great about this book is that it is fun to read. But that does not mean it will be easy. Radically open living means learning how to create *a life worth sharing*. A life worth sharing is *worth sharing* because it is lived in a manner that accounts for the needs of others, is open to critical feedback, and is willing to contribute to the benefit of others without always expecting something in return. It recognizes that one cannot achieve heightened self-awareness in isolation—that we need other people (hopefully, our friends) to point out our blind spots. Consequently, a life worth sharing highlights open dialogue and companionship as a core means of personal growth. The skills in this book will *not* focus on how to take life more seriously, try harder, plan ahead, or behave more appropriately in public. Instead, the emphasis will be on skills most OC individuals find quite difficult—resting, relinquishing control, and revealing vulnerability. The chilling-out exercises embedded throughout the text are one (cool) example of this. So don't just read the text—actively practice the skills and complete the worksheets. Because although the end result is unknowable, the risk of change, in my opinion, is well worth it.

—Thomas R. Lynch, PhD

CHAPTER 1

Is This Book for You?

Welcome to *The Radically Open DBT Workbook for Eating Disorders*. Perhaps you're considering recovery from an eating disorder for the first time, or maybe you've worked toward recovery before. Maybe you've tried different approaches and haven't been successful in reaching your goals. Whatever your situation, we're glad you're thinking about choosing recovery and that you're considering the approach in this workbook.

If you've been in therapy before, perhaps your past treatment focused on control of your emotions and behaviors. That's common among a variety of treatments. However, research shows that there's a group of people who experience emotional pain that interferes with their functioning, yet they have excellent self-control. They don't need to develop more control of their emotions or behavior, so treatments that focus on helping them regulate their emotions or impulses often aren't helpful. What they need instead is a treatment that helps them be more open with their emotional experience and build connections with others.

A relatively new mental health treatment called radically open dialectical behavior therapy (RO DBT) resonates with many who are suffering from eating disorders. People we have worked with have told us the following about RO DBT:

I've been in treatment for eating disorders for over a decade and this is the first treatment that has ever felt like it gets me.

RO helps you free yourself from the rules.

RO DBT is an effective treatment for a certain group of people, but it's not for everyone. Are you someone who could benefit? Read on, and let's find out!

RO DBT: A Very Brief Intro

Knowing whether a treatment fits your personality type and addresses the changes you need to make for psychological health is an important question to consider before you start any treatment. This workbook is based on radically open dialectical behavior therapy (RO DBT), an evidenced-based transdiagnostic[**] treatment developed by Dr. Thomas Lynch for those who have disorders of maladaptive[***] overcontrol—a category that includes many people with various eating disorders. RO DBT, as a transdiagnostic therapy, doesn't target specific diagnoses, but the personality style that underlies different diagnoses. Dr. Lynch developed the therapy to include a weekly individual session as well as a weekly RO DBT skills class.

Why RO DBT? Because It's Not About the Diagnosis

Researchers have found that it's often important for treatment success to consider the underlying personality style. Individuals who seek therapy often have multiple diagnoses, yet there's not a treatment to target all the different combinations. For example, people who have problems with anxiety often struggle with an eating disorder or depression. Individuals who have a diagnosis of depression may also suffer from anxiety or an eating disorder. Plus, individuals with one eating disorder diagnosis can, over time—or at the same time—have symptoms of different eating disorders. This overlap suggests that there are shared underlying causes for different mental health diagnoses, including eating disorders. The underlying coping or personality style can be key to treatment success. If overcontrol is your underlying coping style, then the basic target for treatment, based on the RO view, is loneliness: a lack of secure, intimate, satisfying relationships with other people.

Researchers agree that interpersonal problems are evident across different eating disorder diagnoses. For those who are overcontrolled (OC) in their coping style—in general meaning they don't show their emotions easily, they're often detail-oriented perfectionists, and they can be inflexible in their thinking and behavior—RO DBT asserts that loneliness is a core underlying cause of various eating disorders. And this is true even for those who have chosen to be alone because they've learned being with people is painful.

Long-standing loneliness can be a difficult experience. To be clear, loneliness is not about the number of people you come into contact with. You can be in the company of a large number of people and still be lonely. It's about whether you're forming close connections and experiencing a sense of belonging. Have you ever been at a party or a room full of "friends" and felt totally alone? That's an example of being around people but not feeling connected.

You can suffer from loneliness and not understand the reasons or how you inadvertently contribute to it, or how you can alleviate it. You might believe you're flawed as a human being or that all other people are jerks, and you might give up on relationships. But RO DBT posits that the loneliness stems not from any inherent flaw in you or anyone else, but from maladaptive social signaling, which interferes with or

---

[**]   "Transdiagnostic" means that the treatment can be applied to many different diagnoses, without tailoring the treatment to each one (McEvoy et al. 2009).

[***]   Not providing adequate or appropriate adjustment to the environment or situation.

blocks connections with others (Lynch 2018a). In this book we'll work with you to help build your skills to connect with others, particularly in the area of social signaling.

The Key Is Social Signaling

A social signal is any action or overt behavior, regardless of its form, its intent, or the performer's awareness, that is carried out in the presence of another person (Lynch 2018a). This includes facial expressions, voice tone, gestures, body posture, spoken words, and the like. Research shows that social signaling impacts whether others want to spend time with you and get to know you, and the formation of close, intimate relationships. RO DBT focuses on helping you build connections and alleviate loneliness by changing your social signaling that may be blocking connections with others.

Meet Our Team of Individuals Working on Recovery

We wrote this book with the help and wisdom of the individuals we are honored to work with on their recovery. We have learned from them, and they have contributed to and advised us about this workbook in many ways. Their experiences help us illustrate the skills and ideas discussed throughout this workbook. The bios below represent them, but no one bio is about any one person.

John

I'm thirty-eight, Asian American, with a wife and two children. My ten-year-old son is in all honors classes, and I make sure he's an athlete too. My eight-year-old daughter is shy, but she excels in gymnastics. I run marathons, and my times are competitive. It's important to me to gain lean muscle mass. I've been diagnosed with orthorexia and mild OCD, and I'm concerned about how treatment might affect my training.

As a child, I was pretty anxious. I didn't have many friends. I was a little overweight until I joined the track team as a freshman in high school. I've been dedicated to running since then. I began watching my calories carefully in college. I wanted to be thinner to improve my running time. Then I cut out all fats and sugars so I could be as lean as possible. I allowed myself limited carbs only on the nights before marathons.

I run a minimum of five miles a day regardless—no excuses. I don't go out with friends, because I can't eat what I want to eat in restaurants, and most of the time people want to get together around food. My wife and I had some pretty difficult arguments about it, but she's started to socialize with friends without me. I worry about that sometimes, but I don't want to change my routine. I feel awkward around most people anyway.

Suzi

I'm a twenty-four-year-old African American woman, pursuing my doctorate in education. I'm in treatment for bulimia and self-harm behaviors. When I was fifteen, I developed anorexia.

In the past nine years I've been admitted (and readmitted) to various inpatient, residential, partial hospitalization, intensive outpatient, and outpatient therapy programs. When I increase my calorie intake and gain weight, I become distraught, so recovery has been tough.

All my life I've been a perfectionist. I have thoughts that I need to punish myself, especially after my planned and secret late night binge-and-purge episodes. I lie to my boyfriend to hide my bingeing and purging, and then I feel so bad about lying that I hurt myself again, because I deserve to be punished. He's a good guy, and I hate lying to him.

My parents have always been there for me, and I feel guilty that my behaviors cause them pain. I don't want to burden them, and to be honest, I don't want them to interfere with what I want to do, so I don't tell them when I struggle, and I don't ask for help. I don't feel close to my two sisters, as they are always competing with me. I can't help it if I win all the time.

Amy

I'm an eighteen-year-old Caucasian woman in my senior year of high school, and I've been diagnosed with anorexia. I've also been diagnosed with depression and was misdiagnosed with borderline personality disorder. I'm pretty anxious too. As long as I can remember, I've been a high achiever and competitive.

When I was twelve, my grandmother died. I was so close to her. When I was fourteen, my father divorced my mother and moved to live abroad. I didn't see him again. It's like he forgot about me, my sister, and Mom. I was hurt and sad as well. I turned to my older sister, Rachel, but she just told me "don't be a baby," and to stop crying and showing emotions, because I was upsetting our mother. So I learned to bottle up my sadness and restrict my eating, to numb my emotions.

I engaged in self-harm when I couldn't stop dwelling that others were better than me in classes and sports, or after arguments with my mother. I secretly planned when I would self-harm and would cut in places not visible to others. That helped numb my emotions too. When my mother put pressure on me to eat more and gain some weight, I would harm myself more.

Whenever I think that my control is taken away from me, I feel misunderstood and get angry and dismissive, and I criticize those who are close to me. I say hateful things, and I have an angry "frozen" face. A childhood friend once described me as being "brutal" in my approach to others.

I see myself as an awful person—unlovable and unlikeable. People my age reject me, and it hurts when they leave me out of their get-togethers. At the same time, I've outgrown most of the people my age that I know—they are pretty childish, silly, and immature. They also gossip too much. I'm good at academic work, but even when I was younger, I spent most of my time at school on my own. I felt depressed and lonely.

I saw a therapist before—my mother insisted. The therapist wasn't helpful, and I felt even more hopeless. I wanted to just give up. The doctor got worried about my low weight and tried to get me to go to residential or inpatient. I just wanted to be left alone. I made three suicide attempts, and then I was admitted to a psychiatric hospital.

Stephanie

I'm thirty-two years old and Caucasian. I live with my parents. I work part time at a grocery store, though I wish I had a better job. I hate that I didn't complete college, have never lived on my own, and have never had a date. There's so much that I haven't done, because I've been anorexic since I was ten. I want to be financially independent, live on my own, go out with friends, have a girlfriend, and travel the world. I am so envious of people my age who have friends and are married. I am lonely, but I'll never have friends or a wife, because I'm simply different from other people and will never fit in. My family is the reason I don't have any kind of life—all they do is sit home and watch television, and my sister constantly talks about how you're nobody if you don't go to college. I get so angry with all of them, then I'm really awful to them. I think I'm an evil person. When I do go out, I feel so self-conscious that I just try to be invisible. I don't know how to talk with people, and I can't think of what to say. I'm socially inept, so I stay quiet for fear of saying the wrong thing and being seen as a loser.

I'm having some significant health issues as a result of my severe anorexia. Sometimes I regret not choosing to recover when I was younger. I just want a guarantee that I'll be happier and successful if I recover. What will I have if I don't have the anorexia?

Antonio

I'm forty-six, Hispanic, male, and recently divorced. I've been diagnosed with binge eating disorder. I currently reside in my sister's basement. I was fired from my job. My manager said I couldn't get along with people. I have so much stress—the stress of my recent job loss, my divorce, the lack of structure in my day, and having bills I can't pay. I try not to think about it all, so I stay up late at night playing video games. I also binge until two or three in the morning, either ordering in take-out or going out for snacks from stores or restaurants that are open late. I try not to eat in the late afternoon and evening, but I have to eat before I can fall asleep.

I usually sleep late, and I'm not hungry for breakfast. I don't eat until I have a "healthy" lunch with my sister and her family, and they complain about my lifestyle. They think I'm lazy. I restrict what I eat during the day to make up for the binge I had the night before, because I want to lose weight and get back on track. I live in a high-weight body, and I've been taunted and bullied my entire life due to my size. In childhood, my mother put me on diets, weighed me, and said I couldn't eat sweets, because I was too fat. She was trying to help, but I think it just made everything worse.

The individuals on our recovery team all have different diagnoses, including anorexia and orthorexia, binge eating, bulimia, depression, anxiety disorders, and obsessive compulsive disorder. What they all have in common, though, is an overcontrolled coping style, which is at the root of the different types of distress they experience. Clinical practice and emerging research show that to treat an eating disorder, it's better to address the underlying cause of the disorder, such as overcontrolled coping, rather than the overt problem (e.g., the anorexia). For example, you can see the trunk and limbs of a tree, but the roots are not so obvious. If we were to remove the limbs of the tree (similar to addressing the restriction, purging, binge eating, or other symptoms of an eating disorder), the roots would be left untouched (the overcontrolled personality style). Just as treating the roots of a tree can make the limbs healthier, treating the overcontrol can affect the maladaptive eating disorder emotions and behaviors, by making it easier for an ED sufferer to live their values, express themselves more openly, be more flexible, and connect with others.

Treating overcontrolled coping (the roots of the tree) is a promising new way to effectively treat various eating disorders. That's the approach that we'll be using in this workbook.

This Book Is for You If...

So back to the question—is this book for you? The RO DBT approach is transdiagnostic, and it focuses on helping individuals with maladaptive overcontrol (OC) build connections. If you have an eating disorder and have OC traits like perfectionism, reserve, inhibited expression of emotions, and rigidity, then this book might be for you.

In chapters to come, we'll take a closer look at what it means to have OC traits and whether that fits your coping style. But first, a brief but important announcement.

You Still Need a Team

We strongly recommend that in addition to this workbook, you work with a treatment team, including a physician and nutritionist. While it's critical to address interpersonal connections as part of your recovery from ED, success in recovery requires that your body and mind have the necessary nutrition—and having a supportive physician and nutritionist you can turn to is crucial for this.

Who's on your treatment team? Who can help you be physically able to create the life you want to share—a life that is based on your values?

Medical Experts. Your safety comes first. A medical evaluation with a physician experienced in assessing the physical effects of eating disorders is imperative. Serious and important medical problems are not necessarily obvious. Depending on the results of your medical evaluation, you may need to be monitored by a physician on a regular basis. If you are purging, have a history of purging, or if you are restricting intake, having regular medical appointments to monitor your health is important. Many eating-disorder behaviors can be damaging to your health—even life threatening.

If you are struggling with food restriction, binge eating, or purging (including exercise) that jeopardizes your health or your quality of life, you will need to work with a nutritionist who has expertise in eating disorders. Many individuals with eating disorders are knowledgeable about nutrition. You may be one of those people. But facing fears about food, challenging food rules (such as eating food only of a certain color or only at certain times, or only having one thing that tastes yummy in a single day), and adding foods to a restricted diet often is a tough challenge. These challenges are best done in cooperation with trusted specialists, your nutritionist, and a medical expert. Having a treatment team working with you can assure you are medically safe while addressing the issues of overcontrolled coping.

Working with a Therapist. If you are seeing a therapist (which we recommend), then you and your therapist can use the exercises and assignments in this workbook to supplement your work in sessions.

Moving Forward

As we go forward, you'll notice that RO DBT offers different ideas than you may be used to considering. For example, RO uses humor in a specific way. As you read, you may see jokes, puns, and laughter (*tee hee*). It's all in the service of not taking ourselves too seriously. It's about responding to what life brings us with a sense of kindness and an awareness that we're all fallible. Life is unpredictable, and we can be open to joy, like the kind we often find in humor. It's about learning lightness and flexibility.

So you've got your treatment team. Now what? Are you ready? Drum roll, please. Let's take a look at whether you lean to OC.

CHAPTER 2

Self-Assessment

In general, there are two overall personality styles that researchers have identified that underlie chronic mental disorders and contribute to the development of different coping patterns: undercontrolled (UC) and overcontrolled (OC) personalities (Lynch 2018a). Are you ready to find out whether you lean toward OC? Some of us will, and some won't—but, duh, having a personality is not a problem. Having one is kind of important! We'd be pretty boring without one!

Individuals who are undercontrolled were highly excitable as children. They had difficulty following rules and delaying gratification. If candy was available, they would eat it right away. As adults, undercontrolled people tend to be erratic, loud, dramatic, and highly expressive, and they have poor distress tolerance—that is, a poor ability to manage emotions they find uncomfortable. They are often a lot of fun to be around and tend to enjoy parties and celebrations. They may do things in the moment without thinking of the consequences (Lynch 2018a). Does that describe you? If not, consider the other possibility.

Individuals who have an overcontrolled coping style were shy and timid as children. As adults, they are more rule governed, often with a compulsive need for structure and order; they may be perfectionistic. They have a strong sense of justice and social obligation. They have a strong ability to control their behavior and often plan ahead. They may control or hide their emotions from others and often have trouble expressing their emotions and opinions. When you are overcontrolled, it can be difficult to relax, make friends, and feel like part of a group or community (Lynch 2018a). Maybe that describes you? If you think it might, let's take a more in-depth look at overcontrol.

One of the keys differences between OC and UC individuals is self-control. A number of treatment approaches are based on helping someone with an UC coping style develop their ability to regulate and manage their behavior and emotions. But individuals who are overcontrolled already have high self-control. They are not causing riots or yelling at people in the street. They are hyper-detail-focused perfectionists who tend to see "mistakes" everywhere (including in themselves) and tend to work harder than most to prevent future problems without making a big deal out of it. Individuals with an OC style are not likely to benefit from a treatment based on the needs of someone who is undercontrolled. And that's exactly what we're hearing from people dealing with eating disorders.

In many ways, self-control is a good thing to have. If you're having surgery, you want a detail-oriented and perfectionistic surgeon with a lot of self-control! But can you have too much self-control? If you're overcontrolled in all situations, it can get in your way. For example, when your friends are hanging out eating pizza, and you are not able to just chill—or when you have rigid rules about buying groceries and spend hours and hours in the supermarket—that's interfering with your relationships and having a life worth sharing. If you can't let go and have a good time with your friends, voice your opinions in a group, enjoy a spontaneous night out, or let go and dance at a party, you're missing out on fun and connections with friends, which are necessary components of a full, satisfying life. So yes, you can have too much control. Hmm, I imagine that you're saying, "Let's get to the assessment already!" Okay, okay, here you go.

Assessments

The following assessments will help you determine if you lean to OC. These are *not* measures of pathology. Having an OC personality style is not a problem; in fact, you can have a very high score on OC, and it doesn't mean you have a problem. But if you have an eating disorder, knowing whether you are OC is important in identifying the right treatment approach for you, including whether the principles of RO DBT in this workbook could be helpful. To begin, complete the Paired Word Checklist below, and answer some questions about your personality traits and OC characteristics.

Paired Word Checklist

The Paired Word Checklist (Lenz et al. 2021) was developed to identify OC traits. With each pair of words, place a check mark on the one that most fits your personality *as you truly are,* not as you wish you were and not as you think you should be. If you really struggle to pick between two words, think about which word you were most like as a young child around the age of four or five.

Column A	Column B
☐ Bossy	☐ Accommodating
☐ Risk-taking	☐ Cautious
☐ Unpunctual	☐ Punctual
☐ Chaotic	☐ Organized
☐ Laid back	☐ Hardworking
☐ Extreme	☐ Orderly
☐ Fearless	☐ Think before acting
☐ Misbehaving	☐ Disciplined
☐ Careless	☐ Precise
☐ Wild	☐ Proper
☐ Impatient for reward	☐ Patient for reward
☐ Slacker	☐ Perfectionist
☐ Untidy	☐ Tidy
☐ Rebellious	☐ Obedient
☐ Playful	☐ Formal
☐ Stubborn	☐ Compliant
☐ Aggressive	☐ Submissive

Do you have more check marks in column A or column B? If you have more in B, you probably tend to be OC. If you have more in A, then you likely lean to being more UC. But let's not rush to an answer yet—let's get some more information about your personality style.

Consider the assessment questions below (Lynch 2018a, 80). You may want to ask your friends what they think too. We often don't see ourselves as clearly as our friends do. For example, if your whole family lives in a careful and planned way, you may not even realize that style is so organized. It will just seem normal to plan your conversation or to have a color-coded task list for your vacations, because that's what you've always done. You may not consider yourself cautious, careful, and orderly when in fact you are.

Assessment Questions

1. Do you believe it is important to do things properly or in the right way?

2. Are you a perfectionist—meticulous, driven to achieve, always striving to do your best at anything you try, and pushing others to do the same?

3. Are you cautious and careful about how you do things?

4. Do you prefer order and structure? Are you organized?

5. Do you like to plan ahead? Do you think before acting?

6. Are you able to delay pleasure or satisfying a desire that you have? Are you able to not act on a sudden strong and unreflective urge or desire?

7. Do you consider yourself conscientious? Are you dutiful?

8. Is it hard to impress you?

9. Does it take time to get to know you?

10. Are you likely to not reveal your opinion immediately but wait until you get to know someone better?

If you're still not sure, consider the following characteristics of OC individuals (Lynch 2018). Do you tend to fall on the OC side?

Identifying OC Characteristics

There are some biological factors that influence the way OC individuals perceive the world. Consider the following questions about threat sensitivity; impulsivity, novelty, and risk taking; reward sensitivity; inhibitory control; and processing of details.

SENSITIVITY TO THREAT

Sensitivity to threat is a term for how likely you are to perceive a given situation as threatening. Check off the option below that best applies to you.

A. Do you enjoy new situations? If you see a group of people gathering together, do you see that as an opportunity to have fun?

B. Do you see a gathering of people as scary? Do you get a bit anxious when you see a group of people?

If you chose B, that may reflect a biologically based high threat sensitivity, which individuals with OC often have. Let's take a closer look.

Stephanie has no friends. She values education and wants a college degree but doesn't take courses because she is afraid of not getting an A, which she sees as a failure. She thinks that everyone she meets rejects her as a loser, so she avoids being around people. Whenever she is in a social situation, she feels panicked and withdraws. She tries to disappear by pulling back and being quiet, and she sees her anorexia as a way of disappearing from a scary world. Though she likes to cook, she doesn't cook for others, because she thinks they might laugh at her efforts. When she passes someone in the hallway, if they don't smile at her, she believes they are angry with her.

Stephanie is an example of someone with high threat sensitivity, which means that you are likely to perceive threats faster and more frequently than other individuals.

In general, how safe do you feel as you go through your day? When you're in threat mode, you are alert for danger and tend to see situations that aren't obviously safe as being dangerous. When you're in threat, your body is oriented toward fight or flight or freezing in place. You feel anxious. You're not able to act in friendly ways and you're not giving the signals that are interpreted by others as friendly and cooperative, such as a genuine smile, melodious voice, and/or a playful manner.

Imagine that you are getting ready to go to a party with friends, but don't know who will be there. If you have high threat sensitivity, you probably are not wholeheartedly looking forward to the party and the fun you will have. Quite the opposite. You are likely to be somewhat uncomfortable and wondering what the party and the people will be like, perhaps imagining the ways it could go wrong.

There are many ways that you may perceive threat in social situations. For example, social interactions can be threatening because individuals who have maladaptive OC coping tend to overly focus on performance, and social comparisons. So social interactions become a contest as to who makes the most money, who has the most education, who is the thinnest, who is the most skillful in conversations, or who has the most friends. You can have a fear of "losing" in the world of social comparisons.

Another way social interactions can be threatening is because of fear of rejection. Research shows that individuals with eating disorders tend to pay more attention to rejecting faces (rather than accepting faces) in social situations (Cardi et al. 2011). If you perceive threats in social interactions and tend to overly focus on that threat, it's difficult to enjoy gatherings. There are many ways you may attempt to cope with this. You may spend time compulsively rehearsing conversations or carefully planning what you will wear. Or sometimes, you might ultimately choose to not show up.

IMPULSIVITY, NOVELTY, AND RISK TAKING

How likely are you to be spontaneous?

A. Do you seek out new, exciting experiences or enjoy doing new activities that aren't planned? Do you get pleasure in taking unplanned risks?

B. Do you prefer a predictable schedule, doing activities that you know well, and only engage in risky behavior if it's planned in advance and well thought out?

Stephanie has a rigid schedule that she follows; she does the same activities every day. Going to an unfamiliar restaurant is not something she enjoys, particularly if she hasn't had a chance to check out the menu ahead of time. She becomes agitated if her parents have unexpected guests, and though she says she wants to travel, she becomes worried and upset if a trip is planned, then wishes she had never agreed to go.

Stephanie, who is OC, avoids novel experiences and risk taking. When you avoid novel experiences, you don't do activities that aren't familiar to you, and you don't do things if the outcome is uncertain. You might go skydiving, but only after you research the event carefully beforehand and plan it well. Individuals who are UC, on the other hand, may crave doing something new. They look forward to exploring a new area of town, find delight in tasting new foods, or attending an event for the first time. They may be daredevils who find risk taking exciting.

SENSITIVITY TO REWARDING EXPERIENCES

How easily do you get excited and experience pleasure? This is a measure of how sensitive you are to reward—another factor in determining whether your personality is predominantly OC or UC.

A. Do you often feel spontaneous joy? Are you giddy and enthusiastic? Do you have difficulty sleeping when something new or celebratory is going to happen?

B. Do you see social gatherings as obligatory and don't enjoy parties? Is it rare that you're excited about social events?

John avoids socializing as he does not believe he can eat healthy enough unless he eats at home, and most social situations involve food. He also wants to be in bed by nine so he can be up to run at four every morning. His wife sees friends without him. He insists that he is fine with that, because he feels awkward around most people anyway.

Reward sensitivity is the set point where something is evaluated as rewarding or potentially rewarding. John has low reward sensitivity, particularly around social interactions, which is characteristic of OC individuals. When you have low reward sensitivity, you are less likely to be enthusiastic about upcoming experiences that others eagerly anticipate and you enjoy them less when they are happening.

For the person who is OC, rewards are likely to be tied to perceived accomplishments, including detecting errors, achieving goals, finishing a project. and resisting temptations (Lynch 2018a). At the beginning of treatment, when you are seeing the world through your eating-disorder eyes, you may get a sense of accomplishment when you're acting in your eating disorder, and this can feel like a reward. Stephanie, who feels she has little to be proud of, has a sense of reward when she restricts her calorie consumption and doesn't eat dessert or "bad foods." John has a sense of reward when he runs five miles on Thanksgiving and sticks to his strict diet. At times, others may even validate these behaviors as an accomplishment. This can increase the ambivalence about recovery.

Someone with a high reward sensitivity is likely to enjoy interacting with others, and they tend to approach interactions, even something as simple as talking with the barista in a coffee shop, with anticipation of a positive experience. When you have low reward sensitivity, however, you don't expect interactions with others to be positive and rewarding, and you don't particularly enjoy them. Sometimes it seems like a waste of time. When you haven't enjoyed social interactions in the past, then you don't anticipate enjoying them in the future. So why would OC individuals attend social events at all?

OC individuals have a strong sense of social obligation and dutifulness; they have a willingness to make sacrifices to care for others and do what is expected of them. So while you aren't looking forward to the party, you go anyway. After all, it's a work event, or it's a networking opportunity, your mother's eighty-fourth birthday, or a charity affair. Attending is the right thing to do! This also speaks to the high level of inhibitory control OC people have.

INHIBITORY CONTROL

How likely is it that your self-control is such that you won't show your feelings or act on urges? Self-control includes the way you express thoughts, emotions, and your behaviors. And *inhibitory control* means you can voluntarily inhibit your behavior and emotions. The first set of questions below is about emotions and thoughts and the second is about behavior.

A. Do you express your emotions in big ways, say whatever comes to your mind, and show your every emotion on your face?

B. Do you hide your emotions and not show them to others? Do you carefully consider what you say to others? Are you able to resist acting on urges, if you choose to? Do you appear to others that you are in control most of the time?

Amy was very close to her grandmother, who died when she was twelve years old. Her father divorced her mother and moved abroad when she was fourteen. Her mother, who had been suffering from depression throughout her life, became severely depressed following her husband's departure. Amy's older sister told her that she should stop "being a baby" and should stop crying or showing her emotions, because she was upsetting their mother. Amy learned to bottle up her sadness and keep a smile on her face. She started restricting her eating in order to numb her emotions.

Individuals like Amy, who tend toward OC, have high inhibitory control (Lynch 2018a). They can restrict their eating, even when they're hungry, and they can block the expression of emotions such as sadness or anger. You don't act on your emotions without thinking it through. You have the capability to appear to tolerate distress well, despite the pain you're feeling inside. In public, you don't scream, attack others, or demand that others help you. On the inside, you may feel like you want to explode, but other people see none of that. They see you sitting quietly without any expression or with a smile on your face, so they think you're fine. If you engage in self-harm like cutting, you do so in a planned and secretive way rather than in the spur of the moment.

The problem is that when you do not show your emotions in an open way, others tend to not trust you or want to connect with you. You tend to be serious, unexcitable, and not easily impressed. You can seem aloof to others, distant and detached, and slow to warm up. You may have a feeling of being different from others because of this seeming lack of emotion. And you may not get your needs met, because you aren't expressing them.

What about inhibitory control as you apply it to your behavior?

A. Do you often make decisions impulsively, without thinking them through, and act without thinking?

B. Do you regularly plan your actions, think through decisions carefully, and keep to your planned schedule for the most part?

Suzi has learned that when her college classmates get together, she just can't count on what they will do. They make spontaneous decisions without much thought and little or no planning. A friend who says she's on a diet will impulsively eat candy. Another friend will go dancing because someone asked, though she hasn't completed an important paper due the next day. Instead of watching a movie as planned, her roommate may ask friends over for pizza just because she thought of it. When her friends recently went to Chinatown on the spur of the moment, Suzi made an excuse, because she hadn't planned to go out—she had scheduled that time to study. She was annoyed they were so unpredictable. She carefully plans her daily schedule, including how she'll exercise and what she'll eat, and when her schedule is disrupted, she becomes irritable.

OC individuals desire life circumstances to be predictable. So in ways similar to Suzi, they become anxious when events aren't planned. They have low impulsivity and don't typically make decisions without thinking them through carefully. They are usually responsible and do what is required versus what feels good in the moment.

Having high inhibitory control has its good points for sure. It gives you determination and persistence. You can inhibit the desire for a new pair of shoes and instead invest your money for retirement. You work hard to achieve goals such as promotions or degrees. You can postpone reading a book you love in order to finish a project at work or study for an exam. This determination can help you achieve difficult goals.

But having strong determination and persistence can also keep you stuck in situations that aren't desirable. People who develop restrictive eating disorders (though some may have occasional lapses in sustaining the restriction) usually fall in the extreme spectrum of being both determined and persistent and exceptionally cautious and worried about change. John's strong determination and persistence means he runs marathons regularly, despite the grueling hours he spends in training and the damage to his body. Stephanie is determined to stick to her regimen of food and exercise, despite health issues that keep her from living her values.

PROCESSING OF DETAILS

How focused are you on the details? Do you see the forest or the trees—or do you see every vein in every leaf? ☺ Detail focus is another indicator of an OC personality.

A. Is it easy for you to see the big picture, such as the end result of a big project or the overall appearance of a room? Do you often underestimate or overlook the details, such as the work needed to complete the project?

B. Do you tend to focus on details, such as typos, objects out of place, inaccurate details, and changes in appearances? Is it hard for you to move your attention away from mistakes and errors or objects out of place?

On a date a few years ago, Suzi's date wore a shirt with a small spot on the collar. She liked him, he was an engaging conversationalist, but she couldn't focus on anything other than the spot. She just couldn't believe he would go on a first date with a spot on his collar. Halfway through the date she decided he was not the one for her and wouldn't consider another date. That spot was just too much for her.

It could be books slightly out of place, a piece of lint on the floor, or a typographical error, but individuals with OC coping style often notice details that others don't. Some also have a strong urge to correct what they see as out of place or wrong, regardless of whether it damages relationships. For example, when John's wife or his colleagues tell a story, John interrupts to correct small details that don't really affect the meaning or point of the story. It spoils the fun of the moment. And when this happens over and over, they begin to resent it and try not to tell stories around him. At the same time, John also notices important details, such as when checks are written for an incorrect amount and when there is a change in the car's tire pressure.

§

So what are your results to these paired questions? Did you answer mostly A or mostly B? If you answered mostly B, that would indicate an overcontrolled personality style.

Now you probably have an idea if the characteristics of OC fit you. But some of you may still have questions. Let's take a look at some special issues that might make it more difficult to determine if you are OC.

Special Issues

Temperament is determined by your genetics and biology. But life experiences can alter your coping behavior and how your temperament appears to others. One of those experiences is a traumatic event.

Trauma

A traumatic experience can alter people's approaches to life. One of the core messages in RO DBT is: "we don't see life as it is, we see it as we are." Therefore, it is important to note that someone might start life with an undercontrolled temperament (born more reward sensitive, novelty seeking, globally focused in their processing, impulsive, with low inhibitory control) but a traumatic experience can make them *look* like they are overcontrolled. The fear that resulted from the trauma prevents them from being impulsive, seeking new experiences, and taking risks. The general idea is that once the trauma is grieved or addressed, the person will go back to being their previously undercontrolled self. If you've experienced trauma, then the best way to identify your temperament is to consider what your temperament was like before the traumatic event or when you were around age four or five.

Emotional Leakage

As we have discussed, one of the common traits of being OC is having superior inhibitory control, which enables you to hold in your distress, the emotions you feel, and your reactions to things that happen to you. When a person uses this inhibitory control to hold in their emotions … and they hold in their emotions … and they hold in their emotions, what might happen? … *KABOOM!* Or, wait—shhhh— *kaboom.* (Let's not draw attention to ourselves now or get too expressive!) When typically inhibited emotions like anger or frustration come out unbidden and at a higher intensity than the person is comfortable exhibiting, this is called "emotional leakage" (Lynch 2018a). When OC people have episodes of emotional leakage, it sometimes leads them to believe they have no control and to decide they are UC.

How does one know the difference between emotional leakage and being undercontrolled emotionally? To answer this, we need to ask some questions. First, where do you show strong emotions? Those who are undercontrolled in their coping usually feel comfortable expressing emotions anywhere, anytime, with anyone, and at relatively higher intensity. Those who are more overcontrolled will first and foremost show emotions in private (in the shower, in the car, any time they are alone).

Sometimes OCs are comfortable showing emotions with a few trusted friends and family members. Extremely rarely will an OC be routinely emotional in public, and when they do, it's often due to issues of moral certitude—the conviction that there is only one "right" way of doing something. When one expresses emotion due to moral certitude, it's basically about, "I need to teach you a lesson!" Emotional leakage can manifest in emotional displays, but it can also manifest as behaviors that make you feel out of control, like bingeing and purging or self-harm (Lynch 2018a).

Self-Harm

When a person frequently uses self-harm as a way of coping, they are often given the diagnosis of borderline personality disorder (BPD). However, our experience is that many people diagnosed with BPD and who self-harm are actually overcontrolled—and there are differences in their self-harm behavior from the behavior of someone who is undercontrolled.

As an example, when someone who leans toward UC self-harms, the self-harm behavior is often impulsive. The physical pain can effectively distract them from feeling so much emotional pain, and when the body is hurt, the brain releases chemicals that numb pain—and that's a relief. The relief can reinforce the self-harm behavior, making it more likely to reoccur. UC people are also typically quite open with others about their behavior and readily show their scars.

The self-harm behavior of those who tend to be OC, on the other hand, is often planned or even ritualized as a way to punish themselves. This can be based on personal rules such as the good deserve rewards and the bad deserve punishment. If I believe I am bad, then I need punishment to make things okay. The self-harm is most often for them and them alone, so it is typically done privately, on parts of the body that cannot be publicly seen, and it is seldom talked about. The OC individual may learn to take care of the self-harm wounds so there is no need to see a doctor.

So What's the Outcome?

What do you think? Do you tend to OC? If you've identified yourself as having an OC coping style that is getting in your way of forming relationships and having a life worth sharing, then this book is for you. The information and exercises in the following chapters will focus on helping you develop a close connection with at least one other person by helping you change your social signaling. You'll learn to be more open with your own emotional experience, experiment with breaking some of the rules you've learned to follow about how you or others should behave, and let go of ED behaviors that come from overcontrolled coping and loneliness.

How to Use This Book

First, this book is *not* intended to be read quickly from front to back, although you might notice the urge to do that (*tee hee*). We suggest you approach this workbook with curiosity and an open mind, taking your time to absorb each lesson and how it applies to you. RO may offer different ideas than you may be used to considering.

While knowledge is important, behavior change comes from practice. We'll ask you to try *new* activities, *new* ways of interacting, and to practice *new* skills. If you practice wholeheartedly, really throwing yourself into it, you might even find that you enjoy doing something *new! (Tee hee!)*

So here's the deal. In RO DBT, we expect that you'll experience some discomfort. After all, trying new behaviors and changing old patterns usually includes uneasiness (remember the characteristics of OC?). In RO DBT we believe that paying attention to your emotional discomfort is a way of learning about yourself and from there determining if the behaviors you're currently doing really serve you and your goals. So buckle your seat belt, and let's get started!

CHAPTER 3

Values and Valued Goals

Some of the first steps for recovery include reflecting on your values, asking yourself whether you are living consistently with your values, and thinking about your psychological health. In RO DBT, psychological health means being connected to others, having the ability to respond flexibly to whatever comes your way, and being receptive and open to new experiences and disconfirming feedback—feedback that doesn't necessarily fit with what you think and believe—in order to learn (Lynch 2018a, 31).

When you live according to your values, your life has direction and meaning, based on what's really important to you. Psychological health affects how you handle stress, adjust to changes in life, and ultimately affects your overall sense of well-being.

In this chapter, you'll increase your awareness of how closely you live according to what you think is important in life (and in what ways you don't!). You'll also learn the characteristics of psychological health as proposed by RO DBT, which can serve as a guide as you make changes and give you a structure to identify areas you want to strengthen. You'll use the life skills you learn in this chapter throughout the rest of the workbook and hopefully much longer. Wow, just a few small things to think about, huh?

Oh, and remember to also have fun and chill out. Now and then, take a few minutes to relax, play a game, get some tea or water, or otherwise be kind to yourself. We'll insert a "chill out break" regularly to remind you!

Values

Okay, back to work! Knowing what's important to you—really deep down, hard core, no-holds-barred important (Get the idea? Like really super important!)—is your personal motivation in recovery. Making changes is a challenge. Recovery is tough. Your values—the basic and fundamental beliefs that guide or motivate your attitudes or actions and that help you to determine what is important to you—help you stay on track and support and guide you as you make decisions. Values, when you use them, give your life meaning, direction, and support you through adversity (Markway and Ampel 2018). To better understand how this works, let's take a look at Stephanie's values.

I used to think that the most important thing to me was my schedule and predictability. But through treatment, I realized that my top core values include closeness with my family, independence, education, achieving excellence in the things I do, and cultivating good friendships. I really feel strongly about these values, and I'm embarrassed to say I haven't been living them at all. Sticking to my schedule felt crucial, so much so that I put it above my relationships with my family and others.

My life continues to be about my schedule. Keeping to my schedule includes eating the same foods at the same time, no matter what. It often leads to my not accepting invitations to do something fun, though I hate that I have no friends. I don't spend time with guests who visit our home, and I resent their being there. If anyone interrupts my routine, I rage. I yell and accuse them of all kinds of stuff. I hate that I can be so rigid about my routine that I act so horribly to others. Plus I miss out on a lot. If someone does invite me out to eat, I don't go because I wouldn't know what to say and I couldn't be sure there would be something I would eat. I feel so lonely. I have no one. I know how this sounds, you know, like I'm putting myself in this situation with my choices, but I also don't want to lose control and risk the certainty I have. What if I gave up my routines and still nobody liked me, and life didn't get any better?

Through therapy I'm learning that in order to live by my values, I need to be more flexible and make different choices, such as prioritizing my relationship with my family and making friends over my schedule and my food choices. It's not easy. But I've learned to ask myself, "Is what I'm doing consistent with my values?"

You'll see Stephanie identified some values—things she wants her life to be about—and that these are distinct from the priorities she's held up to this point. Her values are also distinct from goals (which we'll talk about in a little bit).

Identifying Your Values

Now it's your turn. Most people have five to seven core values. To identify your top five values, begin by using the following list to circle about ten values that are most important to you. Think about your honest values here, regardless of what anyone else might think.

Accomplishment	Decisiveness	Knowledge	Service to others
Accountability	Dependability	Leadership	Sharing
Assertiveness	Effectiveness	Learning	Simplicity
Balance	Excellence	Love	Skillfulness
Boldness	Faith	Loyalty	Spontaneity
Bravery	Family	Mastery	Status
Community	Friendship	Moderation	Strength
Compassion	Fun	Openness	Success
Competence	Generosity	Patience	Transparency
Connection	Honesty	Peace	Trust
Cooperation	Integrity	Persistence	Truthfulness
Courage	Independence	Playfulness	Understanding
Creativity	Intimacy	Responsibility	Unity
Curiosity	Kindness	Security	Wealth

After you have chosen ten, go back and narrow the list still further to the five values that are the most important. Make sure at least one of these final five is about relationships with others.

List Your Top Five Core Values

1. _____

2. _____

3. _____

4. _____

5. _____

Now that you've identified your values, you're ready to consider your valued goals.

Valued Goals

Your valued goals are the specific ways you intend to act on the values you hold (Lynch 2018a). Learning and service to others, for example, are values. Getting a degree and becoming a teacher is an example of a goal that flows from this value of learning and service. Deriving your goals from your values, and understanding the value that the specific goals you have are in service of, allows you to make choices and engage in behaviors each day that are in line with what you have determined is important to *you*. There is any number of goals you can derive from a given value. For instance, getting a degree is one way to act on your value of learning, but so is learning to sing, traveling to learn about different cultures, or working as an apprentice in a craft you'd like to learn. What's more, the particular goals we derive from different values are unique to us. You may have the same value as someone else, but your valued goal is likely to be different. Ultimately, whatever your particular values and the goals you derive from them, goals that flow from values are inherently more meaningful and more likely to be achieved than those you might pick at random or those you pick because you think you *should* focus on them.

Again, it's important to be clear about the differences between values and goals. For example, getting a college degree—that's a long-term goal. Imagine that you have that goal, getting a college degree, *without* a value of learning—you just want that doggone degree. You go to class and complete assignments because that's what you have to do to get the degree. You can't wait to graduate in 592 days. You're often frustrated when you have to study to pass a test and you'd rather be doing something else. When you have a difficult class that you aren't doing well in, you consider dropping it, because you don't want a bad grade. You frequently skip class, because you hate not knowing the material and worry about feeling stupid when you can't answer questions.

Now imagine that you have a *value* of learning with a *valued goal* of getting a college degree. You go to class because learning is important to you. You soak up as much knowledge as you can. When you have a class that is challenging, you throw yourself in, because you want to learn. You ask lots of questions in class and seek help in understanding the material. You don't really think too much about completing the degree, because you are living what's important to you every day: learning. Either way—with or without the value of learning—you get the degree, but one path involves suffering, worrying, and waiting to get to the end and the other path is enjoyable and fulfilling, because you are living according to your values. That's an example of what happens when you have a value in mind to inspire you as you work toward your goal. Values inspire us to pursue what we prize most, in ways that give us the pleasure of doing something truly meaningful and knowing *why* it's meaningful, rather than just the pain and anxiety of having to fulfill a responsibility (especially one imposed from without).

Identifying Your Valued Goals

For each of your values, list at least one valued goal. This is all about you—you're the only one who knows what's important to you—so be honest with yourself about what your valued goals are. Consider actions that you want to take, behaviors that are consistent with your values, and events or outcomes that would make a positive difference in your life—things that you're not currently doing. Again, make sure at least one of your values and valued goals pertain to your relationships. Having a valued goal about relationships is over-the-top important—remember that emotional loneliness is the core problem.

Let's consider Stephanie's goals. One of her values is friendship. She does not currently have close friends, so she needs to build connections. Her valued goals for friendship include returning any calls and texts she receives in the same day and participating in activities that give her the opportunity to make friends. She also has a value of independence. While she has already met one goal linked with independence by holding down a job and being able to pay her bills, the goal she is currently working on is getting her driver's license. This will increase her independence, as she won't need to depend on her family for transportation. In addition, with a driver's license, she can work on building friendships by being able to attend more social activities. All of these valued goals will help Stephanie in her recovery from her eating disorder, as she will build her sense of belonging and her ability to be more flexible and open, and also decrease her thoughts that her illness is all that she can be "successful" at.

DEFINING YOUR VALUED GOALS CLEARLY

Defining your valued goals clearly—so you know when you are achieving them (and when you are not!)—is important. Excellence is one of Stephanie's values; for her valued goal, she chose to do her best at her job. But what does doing her best mean? How will she know when she is doing her best and not actually looking for perfectionism, which will cause her misery? A valued goal that she can measure will work more effectively.

I told myself that my value of excellence meant I would do my best and that it was important to not just be a slacker. But I learned that what I'm really doing is trying to be the best, better than everyone else at work, and be perfect—not make any mistakes. That's exhausting! I don't really know what "doing my best" means, because I always think I'm not doing good enough.

Stephanie decided that her new valued goal for excellence would be to greet two or more customers during her work shift, as she has gotten feedback from her supervisor about the fact that she doesn't do this. That's a change, and one she can measure, because she usually stays quiet and doesn't speak other than to ask customers what they want from the deli.

Now it's your turn.

List Your Five (or Less) Valued Goals

Remember to define your valued goals clearly enough that you will know without a doubt when you have achieved them.

1. _____

2. _____

3. _____

4. _____

5. _____

Chill Break   If you haven't taken a break yet, now might be a good time. Chill out: get something to drink or a snack, walk around a bit, stretch, play, do some deep breathing—anything that relaxes you. Come back when you are ready—we'll be here!

Tracking Your Valued Goals

Now for the next step. Let's put your valued goals into practice and increase your awareness of how you're acting in ways that are consistent with your valued goals (or not! ☺). On the chart below, Stephanie's values of family, friendship, education, excellence, and independence are listed, along with the various valued goals she set for each one, as an example for you to follow.

Use table 3.1 to begin tracking your valued goals. Below is an example and you can download blank copies of this chart at https://www.newharbinger.com/48930. First, list your five top core values under the second column beside each day of the week. In the third column, list your valued goal for each value. The fourth column is actions that you did (or did not do) when you had opportunity to live according to your valued goal. In the fifth and sixth columns, choose whether your actions moved you closer to living according to your values or further away. If you didn't have an opportunity to act on your valued goal (this should be rare) you mark column 7. Also, in column 1, under each day of the week, you'll record whether you played and rested that day by circling yes or no. Track your valued goals for the next week. You can see how Stephanie tracked her valued goals below on table 3.1.

Table 3.1: Tracking Valued Goals (example)

Day Did I rest and play at all this day	Value	Valued Goal	What you did or did not do	Further away from living by your values	Closer to living by your values	No opportunity to act on valued goals
Monday **Yes** or No	Independence	Learn to drive	Took driving class		X	
	Family	Hug parents or voice affection	Thought about it but didn't do it	X		
	Friendship	Return texts and calls within the same day	Amanda called, did not return her call	X		
	Friendship	To be able to drive to attend social activities more easily	Took driving class		X	
	Friendship	Do activities with others	Attended book club meeting		X	
	Education	Check online classes	Didn't do it	X		
	Excellence	Greet two people at work	Didn't leave the house			X
Tuesday Yes or No	Independence	Learn to drive	Didn't drive today	X I had the opportunity but didn't do it		

Day Did I rest and play at all this day	Value	Valued Goal	What you did or did not do	Further away from living by your values	Closer to living by your values	No opportunity to act on valued goals
	Family	Hug parents or voice affection	Expressed gratitude to my mom		X	
	Friendship	Return calls and texts same day	Didn't return call from Morgan	X		
	Education		Checked on community college schedule. Goal Achieved. New goal: sign up for a class		X	
	Excellence	Greet 2 people at work	Greeted 1		X	
Wednesday Yes or **No**	Independence	Learn to drive	Didn't practice driving	X		
	Family	Express affection	Didn't express affection	X		
	Friendship	Return calls and texts same day	Didn't return call from Morgan (again)	X		
	Excellence	Greet two people at work	Didn't go to work	X		
	Education	Sign up for a class	Didn't do anything related to college	X		

Table 3.1: Tracking Valued Goals (example)

Day Did I rest and play at all this day	Value	Valued Goal	What you did or did not do	Further away from living by your values	Closer to living by your values	No opportunity to act on valued goals

Day Did I rest and play at all this day	Value	Valued Goal	What you did or did not do	Further away from living by your values	Closer to living by your values	No opportunity to act on valued goals

At the end of your week, come back to the following section, Reflections on Your Practice, to consider what you learned. No peeking ahead now—do the practice first! Take action. Action is how change happens.

Reflections on Your Practice

Great! You've practiced living according to your values by acting on valued goals for a week. (Not perfectly? That's okay!) Now let's take a look at your tracking sheet and see what you can learn.

Were there valued goals that you didn't act on? If you didn't take any steps toward a goal, what was the reason? Perhaps that goal may be too big a leap? For example, Stephanie did not return texts and calls on Monday, and she didn't do it for the rest of the week. When she saw that, she decided that she would focus on texts to start and add calls later. Her revised valued goal is to return texts in the same day.

Was the goal important to your life? Maybe you didn't practice a goal because it doesn't really make a difference in your life. Maybe you chose a goal based on what you think you should do instead of what's really meaningful for you. If you have a goal that isn't something you really value and want, choose a different goal, one that does matter to you.

Was the goal specific enough? Did you define it clearly? Sometimes, without a clear definition, you can short-change yourself and think you didn't achieve it, even if you actually did. For example, if you have a goal of being kind to others, then you may never see what you do as sufficiently kind to count as practicing that goal. If your goal was not defined clearly, then take some time to do that.

Did the goal make you uncomfortable? Was speaking to a customer or returning a text just daunting? There's such a positive side to that! Change can be uncomfortable, so the discomfort you feel probably means you are pushing outside your comfort zone, your routine behaviors, and doing something new! *Yay for you!* You might remember from chapter 2 that in RO DBT, we believe that facing discomfort is the way we learn and grow. We lean into discomfort! If you wait until you feel comfortable before you do something, you may never do it! And feelings of discomfort are just that: feelings. If you lean into them, you'll learn from them, and they won't last forever.

Stephanie values friendships, but she is really fearful of attending activities or groups where she doesn't know anyone. She avoids calls and texts and goes silent when she can't isolate. For her to meet people who could become friends, she'll need to face her discomfort and fears of meeting new people. If she does this, in the long run, she'll be closer to her valued goals—closer to achieving the true connection with others she craves.

When you are considering what to do in situations where you feel uncomfortable, ask yourself, what will bring you closer to living according to your valued goals? Which choices deepen and strengthen relationships? For example, in some situations, honesty, often a value, might not help strengthen relationships. Would telling a bride on her wedding day that her dress doesn't suit her strengthen your relationship with her? Context matters! If you were helping her shop for a wedding dress months before the ceremony, your feedback could be helpful and kind, but not minutes before she walks down the aisle. Remember to consider context.

Finally, be sure you recognize and celebrate those times you *did* live by your values.

Let's take some time to reflect on the positive effects you felt when this happened.

_____

_____

_____

_____

_____

_____

So Now You Know ...

- Values are a guide to living your life in a way that is meaningful to you.

- Valued goals are the specific ways you intend to execute your values.

- Valued goals work best for you when defined clearly, in measurable ways, and are tracked.

- Asking yourself if a particular action or decision gets you closer to or further away from your values and recovery, and whether it strengthens or weakens relationships, is a tool to help you stay on track to recovery.

- Living your valued goals is not a one-time practice. It's a life skill. So continue to practice tracking and living according to your valued goals as you go through this workbook and beyond. When you achieve a valued goal, decide what the next one might be or if you are content with where you are in the actions you're taking toward the value in question.

A Pause for Celebration

Congrats to you! You've identified your values and your valued goals, and know how to put your valued goals into practice. Our guess is that when you complete steps or goals, you probably tend to move to the next task. Maybe it's like, "Trudging on! There's work to be done! No time to play!" You may even minimize or dismiss any recognition: "Who me? I haven't done anything worth celebrating." Instead, take a few moments right now to recognize this step you've taken before you move on. Got it? Well done, you.

CHAPTER 4

Radical Openness

Radical openness is a way of behaving and a state of mind, based on the RO DBT view that emotional health involves three interacting features (Lynch 2018b, 31):

- Being receptive and open to new experiences and disconfirming feedback—feedback that doesn't necessarily fit with what you think and believe—in order to learn.

- Flexibility to adapt to changing environmental conditions (for example, being able to drive on the opposite side of the road than you are used to when in a country where you need to do so).

- Intimacy and connectedness with at least one other person.

Radical openness involves actively seeking to learn about your blind spots, to see characteristics about yourself that you may not be proud of, and being humble and willing to learn from what the world and other people have to offer. You see, you need *others* to point out your blind spots. If you can see it yourself, by definition, it's not a blind spot! You also need a willingness to explore experiences that are uncomfortable. Practicing radical openness is a way to move toward emotional health, as defined by RO DBT.

In the sections to come, we'll cover each of the aims of emotional health noted above, looking at how we can practice radical openness in each of these domains: being open to new experiences (especially when it contradicts what we think about the world), being flexible in the way we adapt to life circumstances and change, and achieving connectedness and intimacy with someone we love and care for.

Learning from Disconfirming Feedback

What's so important about being open to disconfirming feedback—feedback that doesn't fit with what you believe—and new experiences? Here's an example from Amy. Like many individuals with OC, Amy is good at problem solving. She prides herself on helping others. When family, friends, acquaintances, and sometimes even strangers have a problem, or when she believes they have a problem whether they think so or not, Amy eagerly offers solutions. For example, when her friends or family order fast food, she jumps in with ideas about nutrition: "You're not really going to eat *that,* are you?" When others complain about their finances, she gives information about budgeting. And when others don't follow her advice right away, Amy pushes harder. She believes she is being helpful. And she's completely baffled when people don't appreciate her input. When a friend of hers finally told her that she was being bossy, Amy was not open to the feedback. She told herself that her friend just didn't want to give up her bad habits. And she perseveres in dispensing advice to the people around her, not wanting people she cares about to keep making what she sees as harmful decisions.

"We don't see the world as it is, we see it as we are" is a quotation that reflects the biased view we often hold of the world and ourselves. Amy saw her behavior as helping others, one of her top values. But that's not the way others saw it. Being receptive to feedback that she is coming across as bossy, which doesn't fit what she believes about herself, will help her learn about herself and connect with others.

Feedback that doesn't fit what you believe about yourself is likely to be painful. It can be so difficult to give up old beliefs and old stories (such as Amy believing she is being helpful). Instead of taking in new information, you may ignore and dismiss input that doesn't fit what you think you know. This might be particularly true concerning your ideas about yourself: what you're capable of doing, how you view your appearance, or medical advice about your disorder. You're usually certain that you are right, and perhaps you are. And perhaps you're not.

Being open to new information doesn't mean that you accept whatever is said without considering it carefully. It means being willing to accept that you don't know everything, and—shocker of shockers—you might be wrong sometimes! Welcome to being human!

One way we hold on to old stories and beliefs is through what is called "confirmation bias." *Confirmation bias* means you search for, favor, interpret, and recall information in a way that confirms your preexisting beliefs. Confirmation bias can cause you to remember only the bits of information from a presentation, for instance, that confirm what you already thought about that topic. Great way to keep believing whatever you believe, regardless of whether it is right or not! So if you believe that carbohydrates should never be eaten, you'll tend to search for, favor, interpret, and recall information in a way that supports your belief, and push away, forget, and ignore information that contradicts that belief. *Hmm, how might you be doing that in your life right this very moment?*

In the space below, jot down some of the biases you have about which you tend to see information that only confirms what you believe.

_____

_____

_____

_____

So what do you do to learn about your blind spots?

Self-Enquiry

We have a limit to what we know about ourselves. When you get close to what you don't know, you can feel uncomfortable. RO DBT refers to that sensation as your "edge" (Lynch 2018a). That discomfort is a message that there may be something to learn, that you are at the edge of your psychological unknown.

The cool thing is that your brain and your body give you clues as to when you need to question yourself—when you're at your edge, and there's something to learn. For example, when someone gives you feedback, you may experience body sensations or tension or an urge to immediately respond with reasons why the feedback is incorrect. You may feel sure you already know the correct information, so the feedback is irrelevant, or you may perceive the feedback as threatening and defend yourself against it. Maybe you experience a "yuck" sensation after interacting with someone who gives you advice you don't want to hear. That can be a sign that you need to sit with what they said a little longer and figure out if there's something to learn, especially if a big part of you doesn't want to consider that!

You may also notice some unwanted emotions, sensations, or tension that don't fully fit the situation. All those experiences can signal that you are at your edge. For example, if your close friend tells you she is moving to another country, you will feel sad. That's a normal response and fits the situation. But if she tells you she is going shopping for a few hours and not taking her phone, and you experience fear and sadness that she didn't invite you, then your reaction doesn't really fit the situation. There may be something for you to learn there.

Self-enquiry means that when you experience such discomfort, pause and ask yourself, "What might this discomfort be telling me?" Then explore it. Don't accept the first answer that comes to mind. Quick answers are often old stories that we tell ourselves, and we don't look deeper to find the truth.

You can use the acronym DEF (Lynch 2018b, 58) for the steps for practicing self-enquiry:

D Acknowledge that you have unwanted **distress** or unwanted emotion.

E Practice self-**enquiry** by temporarily turning toward the discomfort and asking what you might need to learn from it, rather than automatically calming, distracting, numbing, accepting, explaining, or dismissing it.

F **Flexibly** respond with humility by doing what's needed in the moment to effectively manage the situation or adapt to changing circumstances in a manner that accounts for the needs of others.

One way to practice self-enquiry is to keep a self-enquiry journal. When you experience discomfort, body sensations, or emotions in interactions that don't make sense given the situation or the intensity of the emotions, then ask yourself what you can learn from this situation. In your journal, write the question, "What can I learn about …?" Then for five minutes every day—*only* five minutes—write whatever comes to your mind. This is only for you. As you write, look for more questions that arise and take you deeper into understanding your personal unknown. Be suspicious of quick answers. Quick answers are often old stories that you tell yourself that get in the way of new learning. Write for five minutes for four or five days. Self-enquiry is not about obsessing.

Here's an example: Antonio experienced unwanted tension and used self-enquiry practice:

Antonio ran into Eric, an old friend from high school, whom he hadn't seen in some time. Eric smiled broadly, and said, "Antonio, is that really you? I haven't seen you since we were in the band together. How are you doing?" Antonio, feeling anxious, smiled back and chatted for a time, but he felt tense and uncomfortable. He just wanted to get away from his friend as soon as he could. Eric talked about having his own small company (flipping houses) and a new car. Antonio grew more uncomfortable. Even after Eric left, Antonio couldn't stop thinking about his discomfort being with him: When I was talking with Eric, I wanted to run in the opposite direction. What is it I might need to learn about me, from my reaction?

Day 1: *What do I need to learn about my desire to run away when Eric and I were talking? My quick answer is that I'm a shy person and I haven't seen him in a long time, so of course I felt uncomfortable. That's an old story. Is there more to learn? I was okay in the beginning. It was only after we talked for a while that I felt tense. He seemed so confident. Maybe he was bragging? Is that what made me uncomfortable? He talked about having his own company. That blew me away. Hmmm, I'm feeling tension now that I think about that. I guess that's the next question. What do I need to learn about being tense when Eric talked about owning his own company?*

Day 2: *What do I need to learn about being tense when Eric talked about owning his own company? I don't care if he owns his own company. He's in a business that I have no interest in. I would never want to flip houses. Was he looking down on me? I remember thinking that, but he didn't really say or do anything that would make me think that. But the urge to end the conversation was strong though. I just wanted to leave. What was that about? What is it I need to learn about thinking people are looking down on me?*

Day 3: *What do I need to learn about people looking down on me? Ha. It just came to me— Eric didn't look down on me. I didn't even tell him anything about me; we only talked about him. I was looking down on myself. I felt embarrassed and afraid to tell him that I had lost my job. I didn't tell him that I wanted to leave because I was so uncomfortable with my situation compared to his. I didn't want him to know—I wanted to hide it from him. After he talked about owning his own company, I started pretending, smiling on the outside, but on the inside I was cringing and anxious. Everything just seemed to come so easy to him. He hasn't worked anywhere near as hard as I have. He has a dad who helped him get started in business. I remember that. So unfair. What is there to learn about my reaction?*

Day 4: *What do I need to learn about my cringing and wanting to run when Eric was talking about his company? That cringing was so uncomfortable. What was it? I remember I had vengeful feelings. I had flashing thoughts of something happening to his company, making it fail. Then we'd see how he feels—serve him right. Whoa. I'm feeling a lot of tension now. And urges for revenge. Not proud of that. I remember from my RO therapist—when you have urges for revenge, that means you are feeling unhelpful envy. I am envious. What can I learn from my envy? So all of this is about my really wanting a business of my own. I've really thought about this for many years but didn't think I could do it.*

As you'll see from Antonio's self-enquiry process, the overriding emphasis is on the question *What can I learn from the experience I've had?* The question he started asking evolved as he wrote each day. From the feelings, thoughts, and self-stories that come up during self-enquiry, you can learn about the assumptions you're making, the beliefs you have, and the ways you may be too rigid or OC in your behavior, and more.

Antonio has been practicing self-enquiry for many months. When you first start practicing self-enquiry, you may struggle to find questions to learn from. It may be hard to dig below obvious answers. Sometimes self-enquiry will flow easily, and sometimes it won't, but you almost always will learn something about yourself if you stick with it.

Practice Opportunity

Self-enquiry is best understood by experiencing it. It's not something you can understand by reading about it. Imagine describing the taste of salt. It's super hard to tell someone what it's like, but when you experience it, you know it. So now it's time to practice and experience self-enquiry for yourself.

Practice Questions

Use the following self-enquiry questions as a guide (Lynch 2018b, 31). When you experience unwanted emotion, tension, or urges, consider one of the practice questions below. Write the question that best reflects what brought about emotion, tension, or energy in your self-enquiry journal. Then write about that question and the questions that arise from that one. Write for no more than five minutes a day. You're not looking for answers, you are looking for what you can learn about yourself.

- Do I feel tension when I think about the feedback I was given? Is it possible that my bodily tension means that I am not fully open to the feedback? If yes or possibly, then what am I avoiding? Is there something here to learn?

- Do I find myself wanting to automatically explain, defend, or discount what the other person is saying to me or what I am reading? What is it I might need to learn about my closing my mind to this information?

- Am I trying to deny or ignore an emotion? What is it that I might need to learn from the emotion, rather than pushing it away?

- Am I having urges that I am embarrassed about? What can I learn from them?

Your Self-Enquiry Journal

Throughout your recovery, we hope you will keep a self-enquiry journal. (Yeah, you guessed it: it's another life skill, not just something you do while you are using this workbook.) Any notebook or writing material will work. If and when your budget allows, it can be fun to choose a special journal to write in—a gift to yourself. You can also download journal sheets at https://www.newharbinger.com/48930. Whatever you use for your writing, it's helpful to have your self-enquiry practices all in the same place so you can look back at what you have learned.

Self-Enquiry Journal

Date: _____

Brief description of incident:

_____

_____

Question:

_____

_____

_____

_____

_____

Date: _____

Question:

_____

_____

_____

_____

_____

Date: _____

Question:

_____

_____

_____

_____

_____

Date: _____

Question:

_____

_____

_____

_____

_____

_____

Chill Break!   Get something to drink and a snack, play, walk around a bit, stretch, do some deep breathing, just *be* for a while, or whatever you enjoy as a break. (Hint: Learning to have relaxing and fun times is important!)

Flexible Control

Oh, good, you're back! Hope you're refreshed after that break. Now let's take a look at *flexible control.*

Flexible control is another component of emotional well-being; it means being able to adapt to the situation you're in. One way to practice flexible control is to take the information you get from self-enquiry and act on it in an effective way. For example, once Antonio realizes he feels envious of Eric because he wants his own company, he can decide if he wants to start working toward that goal instead of focusing on getting revenge on Eric.

But flexible control also applies to your daily behavior in general. It means you understand what behavior is called for in the different contexts you might find yourself in. You can sing loudly at the karaoke party, dance with abandon at your sister's wedding, and quietly focus on accounts receivable while dressed in a suit (if that's the expectation) when you work as an accountant. You can also take breaks when you need to, rest when you are tired. A sense of flexible control also allows you to recognize that behavior that's effective in a work environment isn't the same behavior that fits when you are out to dinner with friends or at a birthday party. Laughing out loud would fit at a casual gathering—and it might not in certain work and school environments.

Amy maintains a certain reserve in both work and social situations. When she attends faculty-student get-togethers, she is guarded and stays only as long as she thinks she must. But she's also guarded when she talks with someone she's dating. She finds it difficult to relax, chill out, and be playful in any situation. She's the same whether she's talking with her boss or having pizza with a friend. She doesn't change her emotional expression to fit different situations.

Flexible Control

How about you—how flexible are you? Consider the following questions:

Do you easily adjust to schedule changes in your day?

_____

_____

If friends suggest spontaneous get-togethers, are you eager to go?

_____

_____

Do you have set times to wake up and follow a routine, even on your days off?

_____

_____

Do you eat the same foods every day? Or eat at the same times?

_____

_____

Do you have a different voice tone for work and for social get-togethers?

_____

_____

Are you lively and outgoing, quiet and soft-spoken, or assertive and bold, depending on the situation?

_____

_____

Do you act silly sometimes?

_____

_____

Now let's practice. Over the next few days, notice the times when you are flexible or when you are not so flexible. You're just developing more awareness of when you are flexible. Don't make any changes yet. No need to rush this important process. There's more to come in later chapters.

Intimacy and Connectedness

Having an emotionally intimate relationship with at least one person is the third and final component for emotional well-being. As someone who tends to overcontrolled coping, you may have lots of contact with other people (or not), but you're likely missing emotional closeness and intimacy with them, a feeling of being truly connected to someone else. Have you ever felt completely alone in a room full of "friends"? How does that happen? Being able to form intimate connections is thought to be related to your ability to be open with others about your thoughts and emotions in an authentic way and your ability to flexibly respond to changing situations. In other words, it depends on receptivity to others and your capacity for flexible control. Remember, all three of the components of well-being are related and interact.

In an intimate relationship, you can openly reveal frustrations, fears, or feelings of affection and desire for intimacy. You're willing to share embarrassing experiences, even ones that could be damaging if known publicly, and you're willing to share self-doubts or weaknesses you might feel. You can reveal deep-seated vulnerable emotions that you may never have expressed before. And you're willing to make serious personal sacrifices for the relationship. And guess what? Being open to feedback and responding flexibly will help you build intimate connections. That's the basic, underlying concept, though it's far from simple— and building relationships is the focus of the rest of this workbook. You'll learn more specifics about being open and responding flexibly in the following chapters, including how to manage your threat responses, take down your protective armor and be more vulnerable, communicate directly, signal friendliness, cope with ways of thinking that interfere with social signaling in relationships, learn to engage in novel behaviors, and decrease rigid responding.

Here's the Point from This Chapter That We Don't Want You to Miss

Ready for this? Imagine there's a trumpet sounding an important announcement. Balloons are floating. Add in some confetti. The idea is, instead of looking for all that is wrong with you, *focus on where you are headed, what you want to develop, using the components of emotional health as a guide.* For emotional health, you practice being receptive and open both to feedback that may not fit what you expect to hear and to new experiences, you respond with flexibility to different environment situations, and you create at least one intimate relationship. We use the word "practice" because no one nails it all the time. Remember, being open to feedback and having flexible responses will help you build intimate connections. That's what this workbook is all about, and there's lots more to come that will help you get out of loneliness and build connections.

Checking In: Are You with Us?

Look at all you have learned! Remember valued goals from chapter 3? Are you still tracking them? *Why not?* ☺ You also now understand radical openness and the importance of considering feedback that you receive and in practicing self-enquiry to learn about yourself. You learned about psychological health according to RO DBT, including the importance of being open (radically open!), flexible, and having connections with others. You're learning how to practice self-enquiry. All of these skills are core to RO DBT and to the task of building your openness to experience and your connection to others and the world around you. Many of the skills that you'll learn in the following chapters will build on your ability to live according to your values and to practice radical openness and form intimate and close relationships. Learning about yourself is an ongoing process and a skill that will likely prove valuable for many years to come. Now that you know these tools, continue to practice them even as you're going through more chapters and learning more about flexible responding, relationships, and radical openness. These are life skills, and we hope you will practice them forever. We do.

CHAPTER 5

How Your Biology Affects You and Your Relationships

To best understand yourself and your relationships, it's important to know your biology. Our biology affects the way we emotionally respond to both the world and to our internal sensations. The emotional system we're in (we're getting to that soon!) determines our actions and influences how other people respond to us.

We asked our team member Amy to help us. In the story that follows, you can see how she detects cues in the environment and how they trigger her emotional responses. In the span of one hour, she experiences all five core cues and emotional states we want to focus on: the cues of safety, novelty, reward, threat, and overwhelm, which trigger strong emotional responses in all of us (Lynch 2018b). Later in the chapter we will teach you how to change your emotional state by changing your physiology.

Cues and Brain-Body (Regulatory) Networks

Amy arranged to meet her older sister, Rachel, to take Amy's dog for a walk in the park in an unfamiliar area of town. When Amy arrived, she parked a block from the park and got out. The tall buildings along the street cast dark shadows on the pavement. A young man wearing a hoodie was approaching her rapidly on the sidewalk. She felt anxious and on guard. She thought, "Am I in danger? Is he going to hurt me?"

It's critical for our survival to recognize when we're in danger. If Amy knows she is safe, she can relax and be friendly. If she is in danger, she needs to prepare to run away or defend herself. How do you know when and how to respond to what is happening around you or inside you? Well, nature took care of this. You are born with built-in brain-body networks that function automatically to respond to important external or internal events that are called "cues."

Your brain constantly scans for cues in the environment around you and also considers information from your bodily sensations, thoughts, and feelings. This constant scanning is to determine which particular brain-body network system needs to be activated for you to function effectively. Once a cue activates a specific brain-body network, you'll be able to react quickly.

Here's how it works. The different parts of your brain and body are interconnected through many neural circuits and networks. The brain's scanning device for cues is located in the amygdala (Costafreda et al. 2008; Sergerie et al. 2008) and ventral striatum (Marche et al. 2017) (see the schematic below). Once it detects a cue, it analyzes it. For example, does the person approaching you look angry or happy? Once this analysis is done, signals are simultaneously sent up the neural circuits toward the brain surface (cortex) and sent down to the autonomic nervous systems in your body. All of this happens in an instant.

The autonomic nervous system regulates our bodily functions, muscle tone, heart rate, and respiration, and does it all without our voluntary control—hence the name of the system: autonomic, which means "self-governing." The autonomic nervous system has two main parts (with very serious names), parasympathetic and sympathetic, which act in opposition to each other. The sympathetic system increases our heart rate and rate of respiration, dilates our pupils, and moves blood from gut to muscles and heart. Loosely speaking, it's our accelerator. It gets us ready to go, to fight or flee or take some action. The parasympathetic nervous system slows down our heart and breathing and increases our bowel movements. Generally speaking, it is our brake, helping us to rest, restore, and save energy. Once the brain detects and analyzes a cue, it switches on or off the activity of either the sympathetic or parasympathetic nervous system, depending on what response is needed.

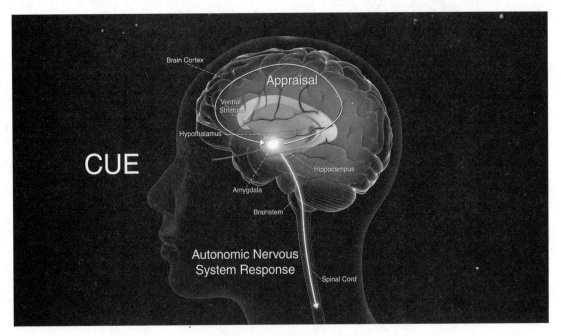

Michael Astrachan (2021) XVIVO

Cues

There are five main cues linked with the automatic activation of a specific brain-body network and emotional-mood state (Lynch 2018b):

- Safety cues

- Novelty cues

- Rewarding cues

- Threatening cues

- Overwhelming cues

Cues can occur inside the body (sensations, heart rate, rate of respiration, thoughts, memories). Your organs and muscles are also an important source of cues. Signals from your heart, lungs, gut, and muscles are sent to your brain to inform it about how your body is doing. Cues can also come from outside the body (dog barking, friend smiling, plate of food, earthquake, beautiful sunset).

We said these cues are analyzed and the signals sent in an instant. We're serious. Your body can physiologically react to another person's face expressing an emotion in four milliseconds, but it takes about seventeen to twenty milliseconds for you to be consciously aware of it. Regardless of what the cues are and whether they are internal or external—or whether you are even aware of their existence—they will trigger activation of the particular brain-body network and an emotional response and mood state. How you feel your emotions is not just restricted to your brain. It involves also your entire body. For example, you feel your heart racing and blood pressure rising when you're scared.

Let's go back and how Amy experienced different cues.

SAFETY CUES

Amy looked at the face of the man in the hoodie. He was smiling, with warmth in his eyes. "What a cute dog," he said with affection, and squatted to gently stroke the dog, who wagged his tail. She said thank you, and her tension decreased, but she was still relieved when she noticed her sister approaching. They walked to the park. It was a sunny day—not too cold and not too hot. They talked about fun times they had had together and laughed about something that happened on a trip they had taken together the previous year. Rachel mentioned the song they played time and time again on that trip, and they spontaneously sang the chorus together. They both felt relaxed and content and smiled at each other with affection. They passed a newly opened café and decided to go in for a coffee.

Safety cues occur in social situations when you feel secure, protected, loved, cared for, and a part of a community. When the safety cue activates the social-safety system, the "relaxed" parasympathetic nervous system dominates your body-brain network and slows down the heart rate and breathing. You feel calm and content, your facial muscles and eyebrows move effortlessly, and the tone of your voice sounds musical. You're more likely to openly express emotions and explore your environment with curiosity. You want to affiliate, to be with friends. You can be playful and friendly, and you learn more easily. Others will detect that you are in the social-safety system by all this, and that will be a safety cue for them, triggering their own social-safety system.

NOVELTY CUES

Now back to Amy and Rachel to learn about novelty cues.

When Amy and Rachel were about to open the door of the café, they heard a loud bang inside. They looked in the window. Amy thought a fight had broken out, and Rachel wondered if a band was starting to play, but they saw that one of waiters had dropped a metal tray.

When something is new and unexpected, like the bang of the dropped tray—novelty cues—we stop and pay attention. We need to figure out what's going on. Is it positive or negative for us? You've no doubt seen animals freeze, look around, and listen carefully, like the rabbit in the photo below.

Photo by Gary Bendig on Unsplash

Similarly, when something new or unexpected happens around you, you may react with a novelty response—you might stop, perhaps hold your breath, and check it out.

REWARDING CUES

Once in the café, Amy and Rachel approached a display with cakes. "Oh, they have Baked Alaska. I haven't had one since my birthday," said Rachel excitedly. "I love this cake. It's my favorite. I must have it." She made lots of gestures while talking and signaled to the person behind the display that she wanted a slice of it. She was so excited that she completely forgot how difficult this might be for Amy, who always considered eating cake with trepidation.

If you believe that something pleasurable is about to happen—eating a piece of your favorite cake, taking a vacation, finding the perfect pair of shoes, or spending time with people you care about—that activates your reward system. You get excited while waiting for things that you desire or crave. You usually act to get the reward as quickly as possible. If the reward is close to you—a nice pair of jeans in a store—you probably won't think about or even be aware of what else is around you. You might rush into the store, interrupt people who are talking with the sales clerk, and push past people who are in your way. You may feel full of energy, your heart beating faster. Your sympathetic system is on, but also the limbic part of the brain, where we experience pleasure.

Think about how you'd feel if you were about to meet a famous person you really admire. You might tend to talk more, and that makes you more fun to be around. But you're also likely to lose your ability to read subtle interpersonal cues or to pay attention to details of the conversation. In this state, you can be quite annoying to others, and you might not even notice their social signals, just as Rachel didn't notice Amy's fearful reaction about the cake.

Oh, wait a minute. You don't know what we're talking about, do you? Hmmm, yeah, the truth is that OC individuals with eating disorders tend not to get super excited or super enthusiastic. You know that high-pitched squeal of anticipation? That's not you. If you have OC, you may not experience this level of excitement, and you may even be tempted to criticize it when you see it in others. It may seem over the top and uncomfortable to you. But it's important to know that when others are excited like that, they might have a narrow focus and not notice how their actions affect you.

THREATENING CUES

Because Rachel insisted, Amy forced herself to also order a piece of cake. When the cake was served, she became tense and hot. She felt her heart racing and her breathing getting fast. She had urges to push the plate away or walk out of the café. She stared at the plate, avoiding eye contact with Rachel. With a blank expression on her face, she said in a flat voice, "I don't feel well."

Cues that are perceived to be dangerous (clowns, meeting new people, going to a party, desserts, giving a presentation) activate your threat fight-or-flight system. The aroused sympathetic nervous system speeds up your breathing and heart rate. Your blood pressure goes up, you sweat, and you are ready to run away or attack. You also find it hard to smile, your facial muscles feel frozen, and you either avoid looking at others or stare at them.

As we mentioned before, OC folks are highly sensitive to threat and might see threat in situations when others don't. For instance, when the waiter dropped a tray in the café, Amy, who is OC, feared that there might be a fight breaking out. Rachel, who is UC, thought a band might be starting to play. Similarly, food—usually for others an important reward cue—can become a threat cue for individuals with eating disorders. Their brains activate the fight-or-flight response. Oh, by the way, when you read about all this cake and food, which emotional state does this trigger in you?

OVERWHELMING CUES

Rachel saw that Amy hadn't taken even a bite of her cake and asked in a somewhat stern voice, "Are you going to eat your cake?" Amy didn't reply at first; her face was blank. She felt numb, motionless, with no energy and no emotion. Finally she said, "Just leave me alone. I don't care about the cake." She thought, "I should just give up trying. Everyone should stop putting pressure on me to eat."

Overwhelmed emotional states can follow both threat states (such as feeling immense pressure to do something that is scary to you) and reward states that are just too much for you to handle. The impact of an overstimulated, overactivated sympathetic nervous system—after prolonged or excessive threat or a sudden, overwhelming reward—is significant. Overwhelming cues activate our emergency "shut down" system and an extreme response by the parasympathetic nervous system to abruptly and instantly slow you down. Your heart rate drops suddenly, and you feel numb. When you are in shutdown, you're a bit like a zombie—you look and feel emotionally and physically frozen. Fear, anger, and other powerful emotions fade away. Pain is experienced less intensely. You feel vacant, disconnected from others, and lonely.

In the figure on the following page we have summarized the five core cues, the brain-body network they trigger, associated bodily sensations and actions, and their impact on social signaling and behavior.

RO DBT Model of Emotional States (adapted)

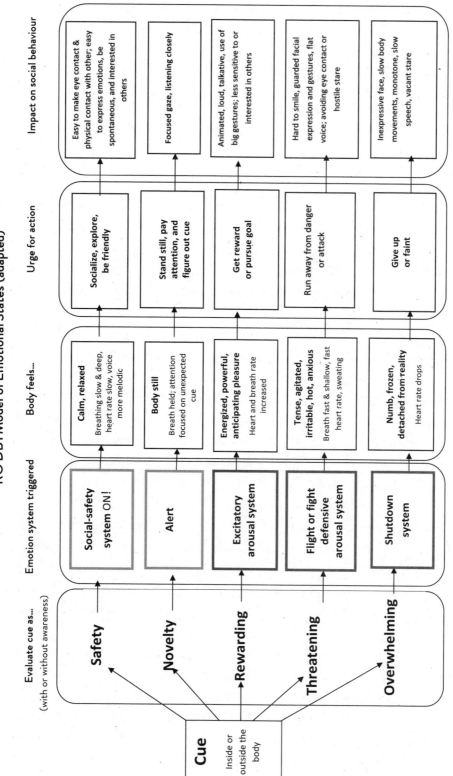

Adapted RO DBT Model of Emotional States (Lynch 2018b)

Now, let's consider the impact the activation of different emotion systems can have on your eating disorder.

Emotion Systems and Eating Disorders

Having an eating disorder impacts your emotion systems. Let's consider the impact of both restricting food and then bingeing and purging.

Food Restriction—Starved Brain and Body

The hypothalamus (part of the limbic system) is the part of your brain that constantly monitors how much energy (from food) you have taken in and how much energy you have spent on mental and physical activities. It is always calculating this balance to keep your internal state stable.

If the calculation shows an energy deficit (more energy spent than taken in), the hypothalamus signals to your body to slow down. That's why, if you are starving yourself, your heart rate slows, your body temperature drops, and you feel cold all the time.

If the restriction of food continues for some time, the hypothalamus sends signals to the pituitary gland (located below the hypothalamus), which regulates the levels of your hormones, to switch off the production of hormones. The level of the sex hormones in your body and the level of thyroxine (produced by the thyroid gland), which increases the rate of your metabolism, all fall. Your body-brain networks are trying to make sure that your body spends as little energy as possible, so you can survive. The energy is reserved for the most essential organs, like your brain and heart, that keep you alive.

With persistent food restriction, your body feels stressed and sends threat cues to your brain. If you feel anxious around food, your anxiety will intensify the threat cue, keeping you in a protracted threat state. Your behaviors will change as a result of these hormonal and body changes. Friends might comment that you're behaving out of character. And finally, if your body is continuously starved of the nutrients it needs, this will slow your heart and body movements and wipe expression from your face, and leave you in the overwhelmed state, feeling numb.

If you tend to restrict food, you might notice that your emotional states seesaw between the threat state and overwhelmed state. And the numbness that's characteristic of the overwhelmed state can often feel better than living in anxiety.

The prolonged restriction of food is putting your body under ever-increasing and unsustainable stress. Your undernourished body can also push you into compulsive exercising. Research has shown that starved animals tend to run incessantly in a desperate search for food (Gutierrez 2013). The scientists think that a similar mechanism is triggered in starved people. Alternatively, your undernourished body might be screaming, "I need food!" and this might trigger an urge to binge—or it might even make you think that you need to punish yourself with a binge or purge.

Bingeing and Purging

So what happens if you binge food? During a binge, you might feel totally disgusted with yourself and think, *I lost control again—I'm a failure!* If you feel a bit of the pleasure that people usually have from eating, this might also make you think that you need to punish yourself. You might think, *I don't deserve pleasure.* These negative thoughts and feelings about yourself act as cues triggering your threat system even further.

You might use desperate measures to regain a feeling of control. You might vomit as an attempt to get on top of things, and that might make you feel calmer at first. However, repeated vomiting has its own negative impact. It can disturb your electrolyte levels and erode both your esophagus and the enamel of your teeth. On the top of that, if people around you have noticed your vomiting, bingeing, or misuse of laxatives, they might make comments that will push you back into the threat system. You might also try to regain control by overexercising to the point that your suffering muscles trigger a threat state.

Whenever your body is in a threat state, the vicious circle gets replayed—between the threat system's responses to your circumstances and the strategies you use in an attempt to calm yourself down—and brings you back into the threat system.

Practice Opportunities

You might remember that some concepts can be learned only by experiencing them. So the only way to make changes in the way you're currently living is to practice what you've just learned: practice identifying the cues that trigger certain emotional responses in you, and learn to navigate threat states in ways that bring you back to physiological and social safety.

Identifying the Cue and Emotional Response System

In this practice, we'll use photos and a list of situations that are likely to trigger different reactions. Some of them you might have already encountered in life (some of them you've seen many times). We're asking you to identify the cue and the emotional state they evoke in you.

To help you identify them, we've summarized the five cues, the emotional systems they activate, and the body sensations and facial expressions linked with each particular emotional state.

- *Safety cue—social-safety system activated:* My body feels relaxed and calm. It's easy to make eye contact, be friendly, and express my emotions.

- *Novelty cue—evaluative system:* My body feels alert. I stand still to listen carefully and focus my attention.

- *Rewarding cue—excitatory arousal system:* My body feels energized and excited. I talk a lot using big gestures. I'm so excited that I miss what others were saying or doing.

- *Threatening cue—defensive arousal system:* My body feels tense, agitated, and hot. I feel anxious. It's difficult to smile, and when I do, it feels phony. I can't look at people, though sometimes I stare. I withdraw from others. My face doesn't show emotions, and my voice is flat.

- *Overwhelming cue—shutdown system:* My body feels numb and detached from reality. My face is expressionless, and I stare vacantly. My body movements are slow, and I speak in a flat voice.

Look at each photo and then answer the questions below the picture.

Pizza

What system is cued for you?_____

My body feels and my facial expression is _____

Chocolate cake

What system is cued for you?_____

My body feels and my facial expression is _____

Photo by Ebner, N. C., Riediger, M., & Lindenberger, U. (2010).

Genuine smile face

What system is cued for you?_____

My body feels and my facial expression is _____

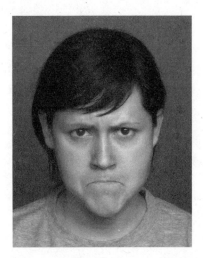

Photo by Ebner, N. C., Riediger, M., & Lindenberger, U. (2010).

Angry face

What system is cued for you?_____

My body feels and my facial expression is _____

Photo by Ebner, N. C., Riediger, M., & Lindenberger, U. (2010).

Disgusted face

What system is cued for you?_____

My body feels and my facial expression is _____

Now we want you to use your imagination. Imagine (visualize) the situations below, one by one. If you know you've experienced any of the situations in the past, try to remember what cue you experienced at the time. After imagining the situation, write down the type of cue you would experience, how your body would feel, and what others would see in your body language.

Curled up reading a good book with a beloved pet

If I were in this situation, the emotional system this cue would trigger in me is _____

My body would feel, and others would see _____

_____

_____

Going to a party where you don't know many people

If I were in this situation, the emotional system this cue would trigger in me is _____

My body would feel, and others would see _____

_____

_____

Taking an exam

If I were in this situation, the emotional system this cue would trigger in me is _____

My body would feel, and others would see _____

_____

_____

Bungee jumping

If I were in this situation, the emotional system this cue would trigger in me is _____

My body would feel, and others would see _____

_____

_____

Taking a roller-coaster ride

If I were in this situation, the emotional system this cue would trigger in me is _____

My body would feel, and others would see _____

_____

_____

Meeting a close friend

If I were in this situation, the emotional system this cue would trigger in me is _____

My body would feel, and others would see _____

_____

_____

Going to the theater

If I were in this situation, the emotional system this cue would trigger in me is _____

My body would feel, and others would see _____

_____

_____

Going bowling

If I were in this situation, the emotional system this cue would trigger in me is _____

My body would feel, and others would see _____

_____

_____

Winning a card game

If I were in this situation, the emotional system this cue would trigger in me is _____

My body would feel, and others would see _____

_____

_____

Winning the lottery

If I were in this situation, the emotional system this cue would trigger in me is _____

My body would feel, and others would see _____

_____

_____

Winning an award

If I were in this situation, the emotional system this cue would trigger in me is _____

My body would feel, and others would see _____

_____

_____

Going to prom

If I were in this situation, the emotional system this cue would trigger in me is _____

My body would feel, and others would see _____

_____

_____

Partner proposes marriage

If I were in this situation, the emotional system this cue would trigger in me is _____

My body would feel, and others would see _____

_____

_____

Graduation

If I were in this situation, the emotional system this cue would trigger in me is _____

My body would feel, and others would see _____

_____

_____

Failing an exam

If I were in this situation, the emotional system this cue would trigger in me is _____

My body would feel, and others would see _____

_____

_____

Driving a car fast

If I were in this situation, the emotional system this cue would trigger in me is _____

My body would feel, and others would see _____

_____

_____

Someone shouting on the street

If I were in this situation, the emotional system this cue would trigger in me is _____

My body would feel, and others would see _____

_____

_____

Loud bang

If I were in this situation, the emotional system this cue would trigger in me is _____

My body would feel, and others would see _____

_____

_____

My mother visits

If I were in this situation, the emotional system this cue would trigger in me is _____

My body would feel, and others would see _____

_____

_____

I gain weight

If I were in this situation, the emotional system this cue would trigger in me is _____

My body would feel, and others would see _____

_____

_____

From Threat State to Social Safety

Have you ever noticed that you can't feel both calm and fearful at the same time? Research has shown that OC folks are usually hypersensitive to threats. Your flight-or-fight system is activated easily, especially in social situations. This impacts your relationships. Your defensive threat response, when triggered, is likely to trigger a defensive response in others. They won't be keen to try to get to know you better or become your friends.

But there's good news for you OC folks: when you're stressed or anxious, you can turn on your safety system by changing your physiology. You can use your body to send a message to your brain that everything is okay. You don't have to try to *force* yourself to relax (like that's going to work anyway—lol!). You can just turn off your anxiety by switching on your social-safety system.

How to Switch On Your Social-Safety System

There are a number of ways you can switch on your social-safety system when you feel anxious and stressed (Lynch 2018b, 94-99). Feeling tense is a sign that you might be in a threat or overwhelmed state. Use the techniques below to change your physiology and go back to your social-safety system. Start practicing right away—right as you read the descriptions of the techniques below. And try them all out and a number of times to find the ones that work best for you. Then repeat those that work whenever you need them. And remember our emotional states are ever-changing and that after you switch on the social-safety system, something might happen to switch it back off. Keep on activating your social-safety system whenever you feel it's off.

FACIAL EXPRESSIONS AND BIG GESTURES

Your social-safety system can be turned on or off simply by how you move your facial muscles and position your body. When threatened or tense, your facial muscles naturally become frozen, and you lose the ability to communicate with others via facial expressions. By deliberately moving your facial muscles, you are sending a cue to your brain that you are safe. Facial movements tell your brain: *I must be safe, because the facial muscles I use when I feel safe to express my feelings are moving.*

You can activate your social-safety system by:

- Moving facial muscles

- Exaggerating facial expressions

- Opening hands and arms in welcoming gesture

- Talking with your hands rather than keeping your arms and hands close to your body

By moving your facial muscles, not only you will switch on your own social-safety system, but you will also help others get into their social-safety system. How? Well, our easygoing facial expressions and gestures are sending a message to others that we trust them and that all is well.

Now try this out, and then repeat whenever you can—whether alone at home or elsewhere:

- In front of a mirror, practice tensing, releasing, and stretching your facial muscles.

- Exaggerate your expressions.

- Wiggle your eyebrows.

- Scrunch up your eyes.

- Pucker your mouth.

- Stretch your lips as wide as they can go; open your mouth and eyes as wide as they can go.

- Stick out your tongue as far as it can go.

- Raise your eyebrows and stretch all of these muscles as much as you can at the same time.

- Now close your eyes as hard as you can and scrunch up all of the muscles in your face—then release the tension.

- Tense and release as many different facial muscles as you can—see if you can find all of them!

Repeat whenever possible throughout your day.

TENSE AND RELAX

Tensing and relaxing the body is one of the most commonly used methods of relaxation. Let's practice a progressive muscle relaxation (sometimes called "paired muscle relaxation").

Do it now:

- Start with tensing your toes and feet. Hold the tension (for five seconds) and then let go and release. Notice how it feels to be tense and also relaxed. Notice the difference between the two.

- Move to the legs and body. Tense all the muscles, hold, and then let go and release.

- Your arms. Tense arms, make fists with your hands, hold, and then relax.

- Your shoulders. Tense, hold, and then relax.

- Your neck and throat. Tense, hold, and then relax.

- Your facial muscles (forehead, eyes, cheeks, lips, jaw). Tense, hold, and then relax.

Repeat whenever possible throughout your day. You might also look for relaxation practices on the Internet and try some.

SLOW YOUR BREATHING

Breathing quickly and shallowly (hyperventilation) happens often when we are under threat and experience extreme fear. Deliberately slowing your breath is effective in reducing emotional arousal. The parasympathetic nervous system will send signals to the brain that all is well, and you can relax. To breathe in this way, purposely exhale longer than normal and slow your rate of breathing to six breaths per minute. Focus on stomach breathing, not chest (shallow) breathing.

Try this: Imagine filling a balloon in your tummy with your breath. Count to five as you inhale, hold for two, then count to eight for the outbreath. Repeat for ten breaths.

Repeat whenever possible throughout your day.

Bringing It All Together: Big 3+1 (Fantastic Four)
(Lynch 2018b)

Now try this:

1. Sit leaning back in a chair (in a relaxed pose). That signals to you brain: *I'm chilled out.*

2. Take a slow, deep breath. Taking a slow breath moves your diaphragm and activates the parasympathetic nervous system.

3. Do a closed mouth cooperative smile.

    - Turn both corners of your mouth upward, keeping your mouth closed. Accompany this by narrowing your eyes ("crow's feet" wrinkles will show up at the edges of your eyes—they characterize genuine smiles).

4. Do an eyebrow wag.

    - Raise both eyebrows and then drop them. (It's a *wag*—don't keep them up forever.)

    - This signals to others: *I want to be your friend* and *I like you.*

    - Friends often greet each other with an eyebrow wag.

Now watch the YouTube clip on the effect of the talking eyebrows https://www.youtube.com/watch?v=ZaO-llc_E64

Repeat whenever possible throughout your day.

USE YOUR SENSES

Look

- Gaze at pictures or photos that make you feel calm.

- Paint your nails.

- Read a book or magazine or watch your favorite film.

- Be mindful of the sights that pass in front of you.

- Create something (knit, crochet, paint, doodle). You might like to create something to give to someone as a present.

- Compile a list of quotes that inspire you.

Listen

- Listen to soothing music (music has an impact on how we process emotions).

- Be mindful of sounds around you (birds, rain, trees, traffic).

- Sing.

- Listen to an audiobook or guided relaxation.

- Have a conversation with somebody and fully listen to what they have to say.

Taste

- Eat or drink something that you associate with happy memories. Chewing is a way of getting into your social safety, and it has been shown to improve memory and reduce stress. Swallowing is also a way to naturally calm the body.

- Have a hot or cold drink.

Smell

- Smell your favorite perfume or try the testers in a shop.

- Burn a scented candle.

- Pay attention to smells that you enjoy (shampoo, fresh laundry, freshly cut grass).

Touch

- Have a bubble bath or a shower.

- Stroke a pet.

- Ask someone to massage your shoulders or give yourself a massage.

- Curl up with a hot water bottle.

- Squeeze a stress ball.

- Hug another person (or yourself, or a soft object).

Remember: it is easy for your social-safety system to be switched off, so we need to practice turning it on repeatedly!

Practicing Ways to Activate Social Safety

For the next week, look for opportunities to practice activating your social-safety system. Use the chart below to track your progress (and you can download extra copies at https://www.newharbinger.com/48930). In it, describe the event and your emotional state, note which skill you practiced and what impact it had on your body and face.

Worksheet 5.1: Activating Social Safety

Day	The situation and your emotional state	Skills used to activate social-safety system	What happened in my body and how it showed on my face
Monday			
Tuesday			
Wednesday			
Thursday			
Friday			
Saturday			
Sunday			

Here are the Points from This Chapter That We Don't Want You to Miss

- You are born with built-in brain-body networks that function automatically to respond to important external or internal events, which are called "cues." There are five main cues: safety, novelty, rewarding, threatening, and overwhelming. These cues, when you encounter them, trigger your emotional response systems, preparing you to act. If the cue is threatening, you are prepared to fight or flee.

- Your brain receives internal cues from your body. If your body is under threat, as is the case in starvation, you will experience anxiety and distress associated with the threatened state. You'll likely have a monotone voice and a frozen facial expression.

- OC folks often experience social situations as threatening. Why does this matter? Other people respond to your facial expressions and body language. It is hard to make friends if you are mostly living in a threatened state.

- That's the reason we described different strategies to help you switch on your social-safety system. Once you do that, you automatically send friendly signals to others. Others find these signals genuinely attractive. It might be difficult to believe (for now), but sending "friendly signals" will get you more close, long-lasting friendships than the shape of your body. Wouldn't it be nice to belong and be connected to others who care about you?

Are You with Us?

Look at all you have learned! Are you still tracking valued goals and practicing self-enquiry to learn more about yourself? Remember, learning about yourself is an ongoing process. Practice identifying cues and your emotional states. And most importantly, activate your social-safety system whenever you feel nervous or anxious in social situations. Try out all the strategies we taught you. All this will assist you to live by your values and be content.

CHAPTER 6

Social Signaling: What's Your Armor and How Do You Take It Off?

Now that you've been introduced to the five cues in the RO DBT neuroregulatory model and you understand that being OC makes it more likely that you exist in a threat state much of the time, it can help to understand how you might have a defensive stance that unintentionally—and sometimes without awareness—pushes people away. In this chapter you'll learn what we mean by your "armor" and how your behavioral armor might negatively impact your connections and feelings of emotional intimacy. We'll talk about how perfectionism can be a form of armor and how urge surfing can help you resist maladaptive or destructive urges and live life more according to your values. We'll also cover three main social-signaling behaviors that can block connections with others and skills to change those behaviors.

The Importance of Social Signaling

Social signaling can make the difference in whether you connect with others or not. Here's a story to illustrate what we mean (Lynch 2018b):

Hunting Dogs, Swords, and Shields

There once was a man who believed no one liked him. His friend said, "Just go to the village and spend time in the square. You will see that none avoid you." The man said, "You don't understand—people really hate me. They look at me as if something is wrong with me. I don't see how this would work." Finally, his friend convinced him to try, and so he did. The next week his friend asked, "How did it go at the village?" The man replied, "I did just as you said. I went to the village with my three hunting dogs (restrained, of course!), my shield on my back, and my sword in my belt (you never can be too cautious!). What might you think happened? The mothers in the village picked up their children and took them inside. The fathers glared at me with contempt, and not a soul came to speak to me on the bench I sat on in the center of the square. My dogs weren't even barking that much! And you think people like me?!"

If you tend to experience threat a lot of the time, you've likely developed ways to "protect" yourself so you feel safer in social situations—kind of like bringing along your hunting dogs, swords, and shields. However, while those coping mechanisms might help you feel safer, they might also contribute to keeping you stuck. In other words, your social signals might push people away, which helps you to feel safe but also keeps you isolated.

A social signal is any action or overt behavior, regardless of its form, its intent, or the performer's awareness, that is carried out in the presence of another person (Lynch 2018, xii). Social signals are ways that we communicate quickly, often nonverbally, and often unintentionally. It is important to note that even though social signals are often inadvertent, they are still received loudly and clearly. For example, if you yawn when someone is talking, it socially signals boredom and disinterest (even if you yawned only because you're exhausted). You can socially signal through facial expressions, the way you hold your body, through touch, language, voice tone, and actions. When trying to understand one's social signals, especially the unintentional ones, we ask the question "If I were a fly on the wall, what would I see?" (Lynch 2018a, 251). This question allows us to recognize that the signal is always something that someone else receives (sees, hears, feels). Research shows when a person says one thing, like "I think that's brilliant," but they socially signal another with an eye roll (signal of disgust), the receiver believes the eye roll much more than the words said. As you've learned in previous chapters, while not feeling connected might help you feel safer in the short term—because you don't have to deal with the stress of social interaction—in the long run, the disconnect will often make you feel worse. Being emotionally lonely will decrease your mental well-being.

Knowing Your Armor (How You Cope and Socially Signal)

The story "Hunting Dogs, Swords, and Shields," shows us that due to having a high threat sensitivity and often being in a state of threat, you might actively and unintentionally do things that push people away. Avoidance might be one type of armor you utilize, if you avoid people and gatherings. Or maybe you *do* go to gatherings, but with a huge smile on your face and nodding at everything people say to avoid any potential conflict and thus stay safe. Is it possible that in your attempt to stay safe, you're socially signaling to others that you feel threatened and don't trust them? Have you ever noticed that it's harder to express positive feelings when feeling anxious? There are so many ways to keep your armor up and to potentially push people away!

PERFECTIONISM

Are you a perfectionist? Perfectionism is an armor that people use to protect themselves from feeling vulnerable. Perfectionists don't ever feel that they're perfect—or even good enough. They feel that they need to strive to be perfect and appear as perfect as they possibly can. Unfortunately, this pursuit of perfection can signal that you think you're better than others or that you think others are incompetent.

Before Antonio and his wife, Sandra, divorced, they fought over many "small things," including whether she loaded the dishwasher "incorrectly." Antonio absolutely believed that there was a right way and a wrong way to load the dishwasher. [Don't you agree 😊? *Tee hee.*] Every time Sandra loaded the dishwasher, Antonio would reload it the "correct way." Over time, she stopped doing it, since she knew he was planning on "fixing it" anyway. Antonio didn't want to be the only one doing the dishes, yet that's exactly what happened. By reloading it the "right way," he was communicating that Sandra was too incompetent to do it correctly and that he believed his way was the only way. Not only did this create more work for Antonio, but it also pushed Sandra away. No one likes to feel judged as incompetent.

URGE SURFING

As you can see, Antonio had the urge to correct Sandra, and he always followed through with that urge, because he believed he should. He didn't believe he could resist the internal pressure nor did he believe he should resist. But it's often not helpful to act on urges. Therefore, we wanted to take a minute to talk about the skill "urge surfing" (Marlatt and Gordon, 1985; Lynch 2018b).

Throughout this book, we've mentioned various urges you might experience—to correct others, over-exercise, give up, pout, stonewall, or punish yourself or others. You may have urges to not listen to others, to hide, to blame, or to not eat. And now we're asking you to notice and to *surf* those urges. How does a person surf an urge? Urge surfing is making a conscious decision not to respond or give in to an urge, impulse, or desire that can feel compulsive but is not in keeping with your valued goals. If Antonio had known this skill and had surfed his urge to correct Sandra, she would have continued to help with the dishes, and perhaps they would have gotten along better. Yes, you *can* decide if you're going to give in to an urge or surf it until it goes away. Yes, it *will* go away. Honestly. As you are OC, you're probably already good at delaying some urges, so this plays into your strengths. You just need to decide if there are other urges that you want to surf in order to have a life worth sharing and to live according to your values.

The aim of urge surfing is not to get rid of the urge, but to learn that urges don't last indefinitely and that it's possible not to act upon an urge. Urge surfing really works! Lets' take an example of fighter pilots to see how doable urge surfing actually is, even in really intense situations.

Fighter Pilots (Lynch 2018b)

Fighter pilots often experience nausea and the urge to vomit under high G-forces. However, if they vomit, it would clog up their face mask and potentially affect the breathing apparatus needed to survive the low oxygen levels at high altitudes. They're taught to mindfully observe the urges associated with feeling sick as sensations that will come and go naturally. Over time, these sensations are no longer experienced as signals that something is wrong and dangerous, and they subside.

When you don't immediately act on an urge (e.g., you don't scratch an itch), it may initially get stronger. If you respond to an urge when intensity is high, the brain learns that eventually you'll give in, and this will increase the sensation of the urge in the future. But if you wait a bit and don't respond, the intensity of the urge will decrease, and your brain will learn that urges can pass. Urge surfing will train your brain not to respond to the urge the next time you have it. If you repeatedly don't respond to an urge, its sensation will become less intense over time.

Remember—you can't stop the waves, but you can learn how to surf them!

Worksheet 6.1: Urge Surfing

Try to notice when you have the following urges:

- To control

- To hide

- To correct someone (telling them what to do or how to do it)

- To walk away during a conflict

- To tidy or clean

- To change the topic of conversation

- To restrict food intake

- To binge

- To purge after eating

- To overexercise

- To leave a lesson or party

- To hit someone

- To walk away during difficult feedback

- Any others? _____

Simply observe and surf the urge rather than respond to it.

Now back to perfectionism! As you likely know, perfectionism is often related to symptoms of an eating disorder. How about your eating disorder? Is it possible your eating disorder pushes connection away as well? Remember John and his ongoing drive to live his life as healthfully as possible.

John had all kinds of rules about exercise and food and did all he could to adhere to those rules. He made a big deal about following those rules even when it created significant inconvenience for others. On vacations, he still went for a five-mile run every morning, even if that meant he missed breakfast with the family. If a restaurant did not have lactose-free, gluten-free, vegetarian options, he'd sit quietly through the meal, "trying not to make a big deal about it," while everyone felt uncomfortable that he was only drinking water with lemon. His children often heard him say, "I'd never put in my body all of that crap that you're willing to put into yours." When he did not eat when they were out, his kids imagined him judging them for eating "that crap." The kids talked with their mother about how he thinks he's better than everyone else, because he follows such strict rules, and he's said that they could follow them too, if they only had more willpower. He also frequently commented that they didn't need to follow the rules, because they didn't have such high expectations of themselves physically.

John didn't intend to communicate a feeling of superiority, but that's exactly what his kids heard, every time.

Do you have rules about food, fasting, and exercise that you feel you must obey? Is it in line with your values to know you might be hurting someone you care about when you signal that following your rules is more important than their feelings?

Perfectionism is a trait that can lead to maladaptive social signaling. Let's discuss three of the five general categories of social signals that can block connections and that are the more common behavioral patterns in the OC coping style. Some might feel more relevant to you than the others. Let's take a look at each category and see how they might apply to you.

Inhibited or Disingenuous Emotional Expression

Worksheet 6.2: How Do I Express My Emotions?
Adapted from Lynch (2018b)

Okay, everybody jump up and down and let's get started! *Weeeee!* From this list, check all the behavioral coping methods you use that relate to inhibited or disingenuous emotional expression.

☐ When people genuinely ask how you're doing, do you say "fine," especially when you're not?

☐ Do you tell people you like things even if you don't, because you don't want to express a different opinion?

☐ Are you more likely to hide how you're feeling, even in personal relationships, never wanting others to know when you're upset?

☐ When you're feeling distress, do you still keep a smile on your face?

☐ Do people ever comment that you're so cheery when you aren't at all cheery on the inside?

☐ Do people ever tell you that you should smile more?

☐ Has anyone ever asked you if you're angry when you aren't at all angry?

☐ Do you change the subject when people ask you how you feel?

☐ Do you speak super softly?

☐ When people ask you a personal question, do you ask them a question back without answering their question to you?

What other social signals do you use related to inhibited and disingenuous emotional expression?

_____

_____

_____

_____

_____

_____

How might this concept apply to your life, and with whom?

_____

_____

_____

_____

_____

What valued goals does it prevent you from living by?

_____

_____

_____

_____

_____

If I were a fly on the wall, how would I know that you're inhibiting or being disingenuous in your emotional expression? What would I see?

_____

_____

_____

_____

_____

An inhibited or disingenuous emotional expression may be pushing others away—intentionally or unintentionally. Let's see how Suzi's disingenuous emotional expression impacted an interaction with her boyfriend, Willis, when he visited her in graduate school.

Suzi didn't want Willis to see how much she'd been missing him and struggling due to loneliness. She was afraid it would make her look needy, and she figured he wouldn't want to spend time with her if she was sad. So with a big smile on her face, she told him that while she misses him, she's been fine with him being away at school as it helped her to focus on work. She added that she's been more productive than ever. But in signaling that she was fine being apart, she unintentionally signaled to him that she didn't miss him. In truth, she was often so depressed that she couldn't type one word of her dissertation, and she was cycling between bingeing and purging and self-harm to punish herself for the lack of productivity. Willis said that he'd been really missing her, but he was glad she'd been doing well. He admitted that he hadn't been calling her much because he didn't want to bother her. He didn't want his missing her to bring her down, since she's doing so well, and he's found comfort with some new friends.

Please keep in mind that context matters when you're trying to determine if your social signaling is maladaptive. Don't be too hard on yourself! ☺ Does your signaling have an intended or unintended impact?

Before Suzi met Willis, she had gone on a date with Joe. She didn't like him very much, and she knew she didn't want to go out with him again. At the end of the date, Joe went in for a kiss, and Suzi nudged him in the side to push him away. Suzi thought this was obviously a maladaptive social signal. However, when looking more closely at it, she saw it was not a maladaptive signal. She was clearly expressing her real desire not to be kissed. However, if she had nudged Willis when he told her he missed her, this would be maladaptive, because she'd be pushing him away when she really wanted him close.

Have you ever thought you were helping, protecting, saving, or building relationships by not expressing yourself or by not genuinely expressing yourself? In fact, research shows that expressing yourself openly brings others closer to you, even if they don't like what you're saying. Come on, don't you feel closer to us, now? ☺ If this is a coping style you use, try out this skill focused on being assertive and kind with the RO DBT flexible mind PROVEs (Lynch 2018a, 379).

Handout 6.1: Assertive and Kind (with Flexible Mind PROVEs)

Ready to be assertive and kind? *Here we go!* With a flexible mind PROVE, you:

- *Provide* a brief description of the underlying circumstance

- *Reveal* your emotions about the circumstance—without blaming

- Acknowledge the *Other* person's needs and desires

- Use your *Valued* goals to guide how you socially signal your needs

- Practice self-*Enquiry* to decide whether (or not) to repeat your assertion

Let's see how Suzi used this skill when she was working on her signaling to Willis. She recognized that she really did miss him, and hiding that wouldn't bring her closer to him.

First, Suzi Provided a brief description of what was motivating her request for more attention from Willis. In doing so, she needed to be careful to use qualifiers to signal humility and open-mindedness. She said to Willis, "Initially, when you went back to school, I imagined that you wouldn't want to feel burdened by my missing you, so I decided to talk to you only when you called me or when we had a scheduled call. I told you that I needed to focus on work and that I was being productive so that you wouldn't feel badly for not calling me more often, but then you began to call me less frequently. I was so upset that I wasn't hearing from you that I could not focus on my work. I haven't been as productive as I said."

Then she Revealed her emotions about the situation openly and directly, without blaming him. She said, "I didn't want to let you see how much I missed you because I was afraid it'd make me look needy. I also imagined that you wouldn't want to spend time with me if I told you how sad I was when I missed you. So I tried to focus on work, even though I struggled because of how much I missed you. Then the less you called me, the more I felt I had to hide my true feelings from you, because I was afraid they'd be too much for you."

Suzi then acknowledged the Other person's needs and desires by saying that while she imagined Willis would feel burdened by her missing him, she now realized that he misses her too and that by not hearing it from her, he might think she doesn't care. She recognized that Willis might want her to share her true feelings with him, as it could help him feel more connected to her as well.

Using her Valued goals of connection and honesty, Suzi realized she wanted to signal how much she cares instead of toughing it out by keeping her feelings to herself. She was also hoping that Willis would start calling her more often, so she asked him if he'd be willing.

Practicing self-Enquiry helped her learn that while it feels really uncomfortable to be vulnerable and share her feelings, it might feel worse to feel disconnected. She realized that if her boyfriend needs open affection, it's in line with her values to try to give him what he needs.

Now it's your turn! Think about a recent time you used social signals of inhibited or disingenuous emotional expression. Use the handout below to try out this skill for assertiveness and kindness (also available at https://www.newharbinger.com/48930).

Worksheet 6.3: Flexible Mind PROVEs

Provide a brief description of the underlying circumstance:

_____

_____

_____

Reveal your emotions about the circumstance, without blaming:

_____

_____

_____

Acknowledge the *Other* person's needs and desires:

_____

_____

_____

Use your *Valued* goals to guide how you socially signal your needs:

_____

_____

_____

Practice self-*Enquiry* to decide whether (or not) to repeat your assertion:

_____

_____

_____

Now that you know how to be assertive and kind, ☺ let's take a look at overly cautious, rigid, and rule-governed behavior.

Overly Cautious, Rigid, and Rule-Governed Behavior

Worksheet 6.4: How Cautious and Rule-Bound Am I?
Adapted from Lynch (2018b)

Here we go again, everybody! Let's shake it out and lean in! From this list, check all the behavioral coping that you use that relates to overly cautious, rigid, and rule-governed behavior.

☐ Do you always follow rules (even if they are only your *own* rules—*tee hee*)?

☐ Are you always on edge?

☐ Are you highly detail focused, so that you see mistakes everywhere, especially in yourself?

☐ Are you always waiting for the other shoe to drop?

☐ Are you likely to refuse to participate in activities because you see the risk or the downside of the situation?

☐ When you do a risk-benefit assessment, is the risk side almost always significantly bigger than the benefits side?

☐ Do you expect others to follow your rules?

☐ Do you judge those who do not follow your rules?

☐ Do you usually believe that your way is the best way?

☐ Do you need to plan for and prepare for everything?

☐ Are you dutiful?

☐ Do you tend to do the right thing regardless of how you feel?

☐ Do you feel the need to correct others when they do not do something your way?

What other social signals do you use that relate to overly cautious, rigid, and rule-governed behavior?

_____

_____

_____

_____

_____

_____

How might this concept apply to your life, and with whom?

_____

_____

_____

_____

_____

What valued goals does it prevent you from living by?

_____

_____

_____

_____

_____

If I were a fly on the wall, how would I know that you're inhibiting or being disingenuous in your emotional expression? What would I see?

_____

_____

_____

_____

_____

John and his wife, Julia, were invited to an evening barbeque at the house of Julia's best friend on the Fourth of July. There were only four other couples invited, and John had met all of them before. John was concerned that there would be nothing healthy to eat and that he wouldn't be able to get to bed by nine—he had a ten-mile run on his training schedule for the next morning before work. Because of this, he insisted he couldn't attend. Julia asked him to please reconsider as she cared about these people and really didn't want to go alone—again. John insisted there was just too much at risk.

Do you think John was aware that while he made himself feel more comfortable by refusing the invitation, he was signaling to Julia that his concerns were more important than her wishes? In session, John recognized that this was not in line with his values. (See the values section in chapter 3). John's overly cautious tendencies made him feel the need to adhere more rigidly to his rules. After all, if he loosened his routine even one time, he might lose his whole focus! But in doing this, he communicated to Julia that his needs were more important than hers. Without realizing it, he was implying that her desire to go to the party was not smart, because it didn't fit with his rules. In addition, he made it clear that there would be nothing even slightly healthy to eat, and he couldn't bear to put toxic food in his body. She tried to help him see that there were some things that would meet his standards, but he dismissed this—there was no way that there would be any healthy food there. In session, he realized that he might have signaled to Julia that he is better than she is, because she would eat things that he would never consider.

Have you ever refused to participate in activities because they seemed too risky? Do you believe that anything new and different is likely to be bad? Would you not go to a flower show because there would be too many bugs? Do you not do things if you think you won't do them well the first time? If you do tend to have rules, is it possible that insistence on adhering to those rules signals that you think you are better than others? How do you feel about people who think they are better than you? Is it possible that you unintentionally signal superiority? Might that push people away from you? If this is a coping style you use, try out the Moving Forward with VARIEs skills focused on helping you to move forward when you initially want to pull away—to take a risk and not let your rules run your life (Lynch 2018b, 117).

Handout 6.2: Moving Forward with VARIEs

Ready to break some rules? Hold on to your hats because here we go!

- *Visualize* the new behavior and describe emotions, thoughts, and sensations

- Check *Accuracy* of hesitancy, aversion, or avoidance

- *Relinquish* compulsive planning, rehearsal, or preparation

- Activate one's social-safety system and then *Initiate* the new behavior

- Nonjudgmentally *Evaluate* the outcome

Now let's see how John used the VARIEs skill to help him with his relationship with Julia, as he truly values that connection.

John first needed to Visualize letting go of his rules and going to the party. While he knew he'd be anxious, he also knew it meant a ton to Julia. He visualized going to the party even though he didn't know what food would be there. He used his awareness of his harsh judgments about some foods to keep his actions from being guided by those judgments. He imagined how happy Julia would be if he was her partner at the party.

He then checked the Accuracy of his reasons for not feeling able to go to the barbeque. There would be a large variety of food and plenty he could eat, especially if he could let go of some of his harsh judgments. He also realized that he could relax his bedtime now and then to let Julia know that he cares about her feelings and desires.

Relinquishing compulsive planning and preparation was John's next step. He had to give up his need to know what would be served, and he needed to let go of his belief that he needed to get to bed early for his morning run.

Before going to the party, John knew he needed to activate his social-safety system to help him Initiate the new behavior. First, he returned to his daily routine of doing the RO DBT Loving Kindness Meditation (more on this later!). On the day of the barbeque, he did the Big 3+1 and he shared his anxiety with Julia, which helped him feel supported.

After the barbeque, John took time to nonjudgmentally Evaluate the outcome of moving toward his values and a new behavior (going to the party) instead of again refusing to participate. While he did feel stressed about the food at first, he found things to eat, and he was glad he went—every time he looked over at Julia, she smiled radiantly at him. He realized that for the sake of improving his relationship with her, it was worth the discomfort he felt. He was also able to wake up at his usual time the next morning, even though he had gone to bed late. He stayed in bed an extra fifteen minutes in the morning, cuddling with Julia, because they hadn't felt that connected in a while.

Your turn again! How about trying this for yourself? Think of a time you found yourself using overly cautious, rigid, and rule-governed behavior and give VARIEs a try. Use the worksheet below (also available at https://www.newharbinger.com/48930) to practice this skill for moving forward when you want to withdraw or for trying out new behaviors.

Worksheet 6.5: VARIEs

Visualize the new behavior and describe emotions, thoughts, and sensations:

_____

_____

_____

Check *Accuracy* of hesitancy, aversion, or avoidance:

_____

_____

_____

Relinquish compulsive planning, rehearsal, or preparation:

_____

_____

_____

Activate your social-safety system and then *Initiate* the new behavior:

_____

_____

_____

Nonjudgmentally *Evaluate* the outcome:

_____

_____

_____

Now that you know how to take more risks (*safe* risks of course! ☺) and be a bit more flexible around rules, let's look at how aloof and distant social signals impact connection.

Aloof and Distant Relationships

Worksheet 6.6: What Is My Style of Relating?
Adapted from Lynch (2018b)

Whoop-de-do! Let's have some fun being aloof and distant! Can you show us how excited you are? Or are you feeling aloof? From this list below, check all the behavioral coping that you use that relates to this style of relating.

- ☐ Do you struggle to show others that you care?

- ☐ Do you wear headphones even when you aren't listening to anything to prevent people from talking to you?

- ☐ Do you play games on your phone to keep people away?

- ☐ Do you never ask for or accept offers of help?

- ☐ Do you avoid eye contact?

- ☐ Do you try to make yourself as small as possible?

- ☐ Do you sit with your arms crossed?

- ☐ Do you smile or laugh only when someone makes a joke you find truly hilarious?

- ☐ Do you avoid looking at people when they talk to you?

- ☐ Do you tend to leave when you are uncomfortable, especially during conflicts?

- ☐ Are you secretly proud of your self-control abilities? And do you judge others for not having that ability?

- ☐ Do you distrust others?

- ☐ Do you delay or avoid returning calls and texts?

- ☐ Do you turn down invitations often?

Are there other social signals you use that relate to an aloof and distant relationship style?

_____

_____

_____

How might this concept apply to your life, and with whom?

_____

_____

_____

What valued goals does it prevent you from living by?

_____

_____

_____

If I were a fly on the wall, how would I know you're being aloof and distant?

_____

_____

_____

Let's take a look at how Stephanie's aloof and distant signaling showed up for her.

Stephanie made plans with two new friends, Cindy and Caroline, to get together for dinner in two weeks. As the date approached, Stephanie realized that they hadn't decided when to meet or what each should bring. Since Stephanie was feeling a bit down and not very social, she thought that she would see if they reached out to her—as a way of letting the chips fall where they may. If they contacted her, she'd go, and if they didn't, she'd assume it was cancelled. Around the time she thought they would get together, Stephanie called Cindy, who was going to host, but she didn't answer. She then felt justified in not showing up. She'd tried to reach out, right? She later saw on Facebook that Cindy and Caroline got together for dinner without her. She was hurt and angry that they left her out. When she picked up her phone to text them that she'd thought the dinner was cancelled, she saw that they'd both texted her on Thursday. Thursday had been a difficult day for Stephanie, and she'd ignored all texts that day. She'd forgotten to go back and check them.

Is it possible that by letting the chips fall where they may, Stephanie signaled that she didn't care? Is it possible that this pushed her friends away? How often do you think something is too much of a hassle and later regret the decision to not participate? Are you not sharing your life because it can feel like a hassle at times? How might that prevent you living by your values of connection? If this is a coping style you use, try out the RO DBT skill Flexible-Mind Is DEEP, which focuses on self-disclosure and vulnerability (Lynch 2018b, 215).

Self-Disclosure and Vulnerability

Handout 6.3: Flexible Mind Is DEEP

Ready to take a leap of faith? Being vulnerable is exciting, isn't it? Let's do it! 😊

- *Determine* your valued goal and the emotion you want to express.
- Effectively *Express* by matching nonverbal signals with valued goals.
- Use self-enquiry to *Examine* the outcome and learn.
- *Practice* open expression again and again.

When discussing the interaction in session, Stephanie realized that she felt even more alone and lonely when she discovered that her friends got together without her. Now let's see how Stephanie discussed using the skill Flexible Mind Is DEEP in similar situations in the future. Remember that we look back on our actions in the past to learn—not to beat ourselves up for what we did or didn't do.

In order to work on changing her signaling to be more in line with her values, Stephanie first needed to Determine her valued goal and the emotions she wanted to express. While she loves her friends and enjoys being with them, she felt a bit overwhelmed by what it would take to join them (shower, get dressed, put on make-up, take public transportation to Cindy's house, worry about what she would eat all day so that she could eat with her friends, feel badly about all those calories, and worrying—as she often did—that Cindy and Caroline are closer than she is to either of them). She had to reestablish her valued goal of connection, and she had to affirm that this was more important than avoiding discomfort.

Stephanie then had to effectively Express herself by matching nonverbal signals with valued goals. She recognized that letting the chips fall where they may likely signaled to her friends that she was not excited about seeing them, which is not in line with her valued goals. She realized she could easily have expressed her valued goal by following up with them a week before they were supposed to get together in order to confirm the details (time, what they would bring). She could have even told them that she was feeling down, and that she knew the get-together would help her.

Finally, in finishing up the Flexible Mind Is DEEP skill, Stephanie needed to be committed to Practicing open expression frequently. She could share her internal experiences and struggles with her close friends while also sharing her love for them and her enjoyment when they were together. She committed to reaching out to her friends to set up another dinner.

How about trying it now? Give this a go, thinking about the last time your personal social signals of aloof and distant style of relationships showed up. Use this worksheet (also available at https://www .newharbinger.com/48930) to explore self-disclosure and vulnerability to increase intimacy.

Worksheet 6.7: Flexible Mind Is DEEP

Determine your valued goal and the emotion you want to express:

_____

_____

_____

Effectively *Express* by matching nonverbal signals with valued goals:

_____

_____

_____

Use self-enquiry to *Examine* the outcome and learn:

_____

_____

_____

Practice open expression frequently:

_____

_____

_____

Monitor Your Discoveries

What did you discover about your social signaling in this chapter? *Isn't this cool?!* Did you mark maladaptive social signals under each of the three categories? Monitor them throughout the next week or two on the chart below, marking Y when you exhibited the maladaptive social signal and N if you didn't. Look how Stephanie did it in the first row. On Monday she received an email about a job opportunity, and she didn't respond, thinking that she'd see if they reached out again during the week. On Thursday she thought about making plans with friends for Saturday but didn't pursue it. On Friday and Saturday, she decided to fully let the chips fall where they may. She realized that only made her feel more alone and further from her valued goals. (You can also download this chart from https://www.newharbinger. com/48930.)

Worksheet 6.8: Monitoring Social Signaling

Stephanie's Week							
Social Signal	Mon	Tues	Wed	Thurs	Fri	Sat	Sun
Let the chips fall where they may	Y	N	N	Y	Y	Y	N
Your Week							
Social Signal	Mon	Tues	Wed	Thurs	Fri	Sat	Sun

Now you give it a try with a few of the social signals you've discovered in yourself. At first just observe, without trying to change anything. Notice how often you use them, with whom, and what the consequences are—both positive and negative. Remember, don't be too hard on yourself, either! What might be there for you to learn?

Are You with Us?

Look at all you've learned! Are you still tracking valued goals and practicing self-enquiry to learn more about yourself? Have you started to practice identifying cues and your emotional states? As you can see, not only is learning about yourself an ongoing process, it can be an increasingly complex and demanding process too! Bet you're up to the challenge! ☺ Try out all the strategies we taught you. As you begin to take off your shields, you'll see that others will feel closer to you, and you'll, in kind, feel closer to them.

CHAPTER 7

Social Flexibility

Now that you know how your armor blocks connections, and you have started interacting in a more open and vulnerable way (yay for you!), let's talk about your states of mind and how they can impact your relationships.

States of Mind

You read about perfectionism in chapter 6. You might be a perfectionist if you believe that you need to do everything right and you are terrified to be seen making a mistake—but inside, you never *ever* feel good enough. Perfectionism makes it difficult to open oneself up to feedback, because it can feel like someone is saying to you, "Nana nana booboo! You *stink* at this!" How you respond to feedback and changes depends on your state of mind.

You can be in an open or a closed state of mind. What's the difference? Glad you asked. When you're in open mind state, you embrace new information; listen, reflect, and learn from feedback; and adjust to an ever-changing world. Of course, this doesn't mean you always *accept* the feedback or that everyone should go around constantly giving feedback. When you have a closed mind, you block new information, rigidly stick to your own beliefs and opinions, disregard feedback, and refute the possibility of any new learning or change. Why does it matter? Because a closed mind state can keep you stuck in a rut and alienate you from others. It can stop you from learning and growing. It can even be dangerous, if you don't listen to important information about possible risks.

When you feel threatened, you're even more likely to close off your mind (Vansteenwegen et al. 2008; Lynch 2018a). It's all about protection. Threat evokes in all of us the need to defend and fight or flee. OC folks are prone to perceive events and people as threatening, hence they will relate to the world from a closed mind more often. And threats can come in many forms—novel, unpredictable situations (surprise parties—*shudder*), new ideas (your boss decides to reorganize your workplace), being criticized for being quiet. Oh yeah, but we still haven't told you the two *types* of closed mind. Let's take a look at them!

Fixed Mind

Imagine that you're piloting a ship in the Antarctic. Suddenly, a huge iceberg looms out of the fog, right in front you. You're afraid, but at the same time, you firmly believe that your ship is indestructible. You're so sure of it that you don't consider other possibilities. So you sail ahead with full power, thinking, *I can break right through this iceberg! No need to change course!* Of course, remember what happened on the "unsinkable" *Titanic*'s first (and only) journey (Lynch 2018b, 233-253)?

How do you react when there are icebergs in the way of your recovery or achieving your valued goals? (No, not *real* icebergs, but obstacles you encounter.) Are you open to input from others when their ideas differ from yours?

When you think you know all the answers (hmm, does the term "know it all" come to mind?), that change is unnecessary, and that you don't need to consider feedback or suggestions from others, that's called "fixed mind." In fixed mind, you stubbornly defend your opinions, beliefs, and actions. You are right, and they are wrong. Period. *You're* not the one who needs to change! It's *those others* who need to change! *Your* position is righteous. All of us go to fixed mind-set from time to time (some more often than others) (Lynch 2018b, 233-253).

Sometimes fixed mind can be useful, as it's our "fighter." It protects us from doubts and ambivalence, or when we must defend ourselves, for instance, soldiers in war. With fixed mind, you feel confident and less anxious in situations where there is a lot of uncertainty and unpredictability. But in most situations, fixed mind keeps you stuck and doesn't allow you to learn from feedback and change. Fixed mind also can negatively impact your relationships. Let's see Stephanie's example:

Stephanie was having lunch with a couple of friends from the eating disorder support group. Her friend Suzi said, "Hey, Steph, I'm a little worried about you. You're not eating much, and you look thinner. Have you thought about asking your therapist about a higher level of care?" Stephanie responded, "That's ridiculous! I'm fine! You don't have a clue! There is no way I am stepping up my treatment!" Suzi said, "I'm sorry. But know that I asked only because I'm worried. And you're one of my best friends—I really care about you." Stephanie then went silent and did not say anything to anyone for the rest of the lunch.

Let's take a look at another example of fixed mind and how it impacted John and his family on his daughter's birthday:

Since the kids were young, John's family enjoyed a tradition of birthday breakfasts. The birthday person would pick what they wanted to eat, and the family would cook it together. As the kids got older and John got more into his exercise, John decided that the kids were old enough that they probably no longer cared about that tradition. He started getting up early to run, even on the kids' birthdays. The first time he did that, his wife, Julia, told him that they had waited an hour and then ate without him. John said he'd just lost track of time. The next year, on the eve of his daughter's birthday, John set his alarm for his morning run. Julia noticed this and decided to give him some feedback (she also knew he was learning RO). She said, "I noticed you set the alarm. Honey, it's Katie's birthday, and we have her birthday breakfast planned. Can you please skip your run for one day and have a breakfast with us? I'm asking because it's her birthday. We miss you, and we wish you would stay home to be with us." John felt threatened by the request not to run, and he felt badly to hear the feedback that his family missed him. He responded, "I need to run to feel like I can relax and enjoy the day with the family. I don't really eat breakfast anyway, so it doesn't really matter." Julia said, "Even if you don't eat with us, we just want you to be with us." John felt worse and, with irritation in his voice, said, "I'm only going eight miles tomorrow. I'll be back before you know it."

As you can see, fixed mind usually comes with feelings of irritation, frustration, or anger, because you think it's wrong that others are questioning your point of view (Lynch 2018b). You have an urge to defend your view, because others are mistaken. You know what is the right rule and right answer. If they push back at all, you can get numb and frozen and completely stop interacting with them, because there's nothing they can say that you're willing to listen to.

Loosening the Grip of Fixed Mind

Fixed mind can be tricky. You often don't know when you're in it. You may just think you're right. In the handout below we have outlined a few steps that you can take to help yourself recognize and acknowledge that you are in fixed mind.

Important note! It's not possible to *force* yourself out of fixed mind. And blaming yourself for your fixed mind isn't helpful. Those approaches just don't work. But if you activate your social-safety system and treat yourself with kindness, it's likely that you'll be more open to new information. Remember, no one is correct all the time (not even you or me) and feeling threatened is linked with closed mind. So if your social-safety system is activated, it is more likely that you will loosen the grip of fixed mind.

PRACTICE OPPORTUNITY

Think about a recent time when you found it difficult to let go of your perspective and consider another point of view. Got one? Great! Now use handout 7.1 to learn how to loosen the grip of fixed mind (adapted from Lynch 2018b).

Handout 7.1: Loosening the Grip of Fixed Mind

Step 1: When feeling psychologically threatened, observe emotions, urges for action, and thoughts that may be linked to fixed mind. Ask yourself:

- Are you feeling irritated, nervous, angry, numb, or empty?

- Do you have urges to defend yourself or ignore what is happening?

- Do you think that it is wrong for others to question your point of view?

- Are you confident that you know the answer or that the other person is wrong?

Step 2: Acknowledge the possibility of being in fixed mind.

- Acknowledge that physical tension in the body means you feel threatened.

- Acknowledge that you are fighting or resisting something without mindlessly letting go of your point of view.

- Gently remember: when in fixed mind, your thoughts, emotions, urges, and sensations are determined by your past experiences.

- Remind yourself that fixed mind alerts us to those things in our life we need to be more open to, to improve ourselves or learn.

Step 3: Don't try to *fix* fixed mind. Be kind instead.

- Practice being open to what is happening in this moment. Let go of assuming you have the correct answer. Encourage yourself to stay open to the feedback. (See also chapter 11.) Consider that you might be sticking to your rules, even when this pushes people away.

- Change physiology:

  - Use Big 3+1: closed-mouth smile while breathing deeply, use eyebrow wags.

  - Use a loving-kindness practice (more on this in chapter 12) by repeating silently to yourself: *May my fixed mind find peace; may my fixed mind be content; may my fixed mind be safe and secure.*

- Rather than resisting, fixing, or defending your fixed mind, allow it to simply *be*. Trying to control fixed mind is like criticizing yourself for being too self-critical—it just doesn't work.

- Forgive yourself for being in fixed mind; remember that we all have a fixed mind.

- Take a courageous step of going opposite to fixed mind. Try to laugh at your imperfections and stay open to different perspectives.

Let's go back to Stephanie.

Later that afternoon, when she left her friends, Stephanie reflected and asked herself, "Was I in fixed mind?" She looked at handout 7.1, Loosening the Grip of Fixed Mind. She recognized that she was irritated and angry with Suzi's comment. She acknowledged that she'd been defensive and refused to even consider that Suzi had a point. She didn't want to face that her eating had been slipping lately—she'd been restricting her food and hadn't been following her nutritionist's meal plan. She remembered that when you're in fixed mind that alerts you that there are things you need to be more open about. She decided to do the loving-kindness meditation and be kind to herself, forgiving herself for being in fixed mind. She didn't think she needed more but decided to consider that she might be wrong and ask for opinions that she trusted. She phoned her therapist, explained everything, and asked her opinion about more support. She then called Suzi to thank her for giving her some difficult feedback and for being an honest, caring, and trustworthy friend.

Fatalistic Mind

If fixed mind is digging in your heels to defend your position, then the other closed mind-set, fatalistic mind, is throwing your hands up in the air. Fixed mind says that change is unnecessary because you know all the answers, fatalistic mind says that change is impossible, problems are unsolvable, and there are no answers. If fatalistic mind were the captain of the *Titanic*, after hitting the iceberg, he'd retreat to his cabin, lock the door, and refuse to help his crew launch lifeboats—the disaster has happened, and nothing can make it better (Lynch 2018b, 233-253). Let's look at Stephanie's example.

Stephanie has always wanted to return to college, but she has been afraid she'd fail. She was talking with her mom about it one night, and her mom said, "You're so smart, and I know if you really gave it effort, you could do whatever you want." Stephanie felt overwhelmed at the thought of it: "Mom, you know I'm not the type of person who can just decide to do something like that. You think I'm smart only because you're my mom. I'll never be good enough to get the grades I'd want. It'd only cause me more stress." Her mom smiled: "I really believe in you." Stephanie looked at her and said, "Sure, Mom, I'll think about it," knowing full well she had no intention of giving it another thought.

Fatalistic mind is an escape artist, especially when you don't want to take responsibility for your actions. While fixed mind puts up vigorous resistance to challenging feedback, fatalistic mind gives up and shuts down when you don't get what you want or when you feel overwhelmed. Instead of fighting or resisting, fatalistic mind gets you to abandon hope and withdraw from a situation, fooling you into believing that you have good reasons to do so and that you're not just avoiding it. Fatalistic mind can lead you to behave in a way that can be best described as shooting yourself in the foot. Sometimes you can flip from one closed mind to another, from firmly resisting to suddenly giving up. And sometimes you can get very *fixed* about not acknowledging that you're in fatalistic mind.

However, fatalistic mind does not always mean that you are necessarily doing anything wrong—you may be working too hard and need a rest. The truth is that at least sometimes you need to rest or to reward yourself for hard work. This is a part of healthy living and taking care of yourself. Only if you can take good care of yourself, will you be in good position to help others.

PRACTICE OPPORTUNITY

Think of a recent time when you were in fatalistic mind and then complete the exercise below.

Check the following statements or thoughts that you had:

- It will never work.

- Why bother.

- Can't do it.

- I don't care.

- Whatever.

- Yes, but it didn't work last time.

- Nothing's going to fix me.

- This book won't fix me.

Do you have these thoughts when you hear unwelcome feedback or feel frightened about a situation? Are there any other thoughts that you have about giving up?

_____

_____

_____

_____

_____

_____

_____

And now consider these two statements and then describe situations when this happened in your life:

- "I found myself thinking that others should change first—or at least admit they may have made a mistake—before I should consider doing the same."

_____

_____

_____

- "I was secretly hoping that by blaming myself, the other person would stop giving me feedback."

_____

_____

_____

Learning from Fatalistic Mind

Handout 7.2, Learning from Fatalistic Mind, gives you the steps to take when you find you are in fatalistic mind (Lynch 2018b).

Handout 7.2: Learning from Fatalistic Mind

Step 1: Observe emotions, urges, and thoughts that may be linked to fatalistic mind. Does any statement below apply to you?

- I feel unappreciated, misunderstood, helpless, offended, sulky, pessimistic, or numbed.

- Change is impossible ("Why bother?"); others must change first before I can.

- Everything will be fine; this problem will disappear, despite repeated feedback that this is a serious problem.

- I have urges to punish anyone suggesting that I should change. I want to pout, cry, walk away, or deny. I make unrealistic promises that I will change just to stop others from giving me feedback.

Step 2: Acknowledge the possibility of being in fatalistic mind (remember that fatalistic mind is the opposite of resisting or fighting).

- Acknowledge that you want to give up. Remember that fatalistic mind is your escape artist. It fools you into thinking that you should give up and refuse to admit you're avoiding something.

- Fatalistic mind is not always "bad." Fatalistic mind can help you recognize times when you are pushing yourself too hard and when you need take a rest.

Step 3: Listen and learn from fatalistic mind by using the skills below to surf the urge to give up, pout, or punish others.

- Take the first step by acknowledging that you are choosing to operate from fatalistic mind—no one can force you to behave this way.

- Go opposite to desires to numb out or give up. Be present.

- Let go of longing for the world to change or secretly hoping that the problem will go away. Accept responsibility for creating your own reality.

- Stop blaming others for "making" you miserable and admit to yourself (and others) how you're contributing to the problem.

- Fatalistic mind thrives on secrecy. Reveal to the other person your urges to stonewall or give up.

- If fatalistic mind is signaling that you're working too hard, take a break.

- Change your physiology to feel more socially safe by using Big 3+1 while thinking about the problem or feedback that your fatalistic mind has labeled as unsolvable.

- Turn your mind to the possibility of change.

- Clarify the steps needed to solve the problem—and then take the first step.

- Focus on mindfully taking one step at a time.

- **Remember that rejecting help from others keeps you stuck in fatalistic mind. Practice allowing others to help you.**

- Forgive yourself for being in fatalistic mind.

Let's see how Stephanie used this skill with her thoughts about going to college.

The first thing Stephanie did was realize that she believed that change was impossible. There was no point to trying, because no matter what she did, she thought she would fail. She saw that she was thinking, "Why bother?" and that she didn't want to risk being embarrassed by failure at college.

Next Stephanie had to acknowledge the possibility that she was in fatalistic mind. She remembered that fatalistic mind is her escape artist, and it could fool her into thinking that she should give up and not admit that she's avoiding something.

Stephanie then acknowledged that she was choosing to operate from fatalistic mind, remembering that no one can force her to behave this way. She went opposite to her desires to give up. She had to let go of secretly hoping that the problem would go away so that she could accept responsibility for creating her own reality. This even helped her feel a bit empowered! She realized she had to stop blaming her parents for not allowing her to go back to college after first semester when she was eighteen because she was so impaired by her anorexia. She went opposite to blaming others by admitting to herself and eventually to her mother how she was and still is contributing to the problem of her not having a college degree. She told her mom that she realizes if she is going to go back to school, she has to do it for herself. Because she knew that fatalistic mind thrives on secrecy, she revealed to her mom her urges to give up on this and admitted that while those urges are strong, so was her desire to finish school. Stephanie changed her physiology to feel more socially safe and less anxious by using Big 3+1 while thinking about the idea of going back to college. Stephanie turned her mind to the possibility of change.

Stephanie then decided the next steps she needed to take in order to get to school. She needed to decide where to go and then she needed to apply. Stephanie knew she wanted to be close to home, as her parents were her greatest support. Mindfully, Stephanie decided to begin by looking at the colleges or universities within a two-hour drive from home. Her parents offered to help her pay for school and, while she wanted to refuse due to her value of independence, she realized that rejecting help from her parents would keep her stuck in fatalistic mind. She knew she had to practice allowing others to help her, even though—and especially when—it felt uncomfortable to do so. Finally, Stephanie needed to forgive herself for being in fatalistic mind in the first place.

PRACTICE OPPORTUNITY

Now it's your turn. While thinking of a recent time when you were in fatalistic mind, use handout 7.2 (Learning from Fatalistic Mind) to identify and learn from fatalistic mind. Go through each step fully and notice any changes in your thinking, sensations, and emotions.

Flexible Mind

Now that you have learned about the two types of closed mind, let's explore flexible mind. Flexible mind is the essence of radical openness and exploration (Lynch 2018b, 243-248). So let's go back to the first scenario—you're the captain of a ship and there's an iceberg. With flexible mind, you'll change course and reduce the speed. Even if it hits, you won't abandon the ship when passengers are in trouble or vigorously insist, "It's my way or the highway!" In flexible mind, you openly listen to feedback without immediately refuting what they're saying. Flexible mind is willing to experience new things with an open heart, without losing track of your values. Flexible mind understands that we don't see the world as it is—we see it as *we* are. Let's look at Antonio's example.

Antonio was talking to his mother, Maria, on the phone. Maria asked what was wrong with Daniel, Antonio's son, because he hadn't called her in months. You see, Maria is OC too, and she firmly believes that grandkids should call their grandmother, but that grandmothers don't have to call their grandkids.

Antonio said, "Well, Mom, sometimes when you talk to people, you might unintentionally signal harsh disapproval, and they might feel belittled." (Perhaps Antonio also needed to learn a bit more about how he might socially signal!) His mother huffed, "Well, that's a low blow!" (What mind state does this sound like?) Antonio then realized that what he said likely signaled judgment. He said, "I am sorry, Mom. I didn't mean to sound judgmental. I thought you were asking why Daniel might not have been calling." Maria responded, "Well, I'll just never say anything ever again!" (What mind state does this sound like?) Antonio teased, "Not only do I not want that, but I also don't think it would be possible. I am truly sorry, Mom. I didn't mean to upset you. Would you prefer if I stopped giving you feedback?" His mom then took a deep breath and let out a long sigh. She responded slowly, "Well, I guess sometimes I might unintentionally make people feel like they're being judged when I talk with them." To which Antonio responded, "Hello, flexible mind!"

Finding Flexible Mind

To find flexible mind, the following tips can help (Lynch 2018b, 243-248):

- Turn your mind to the possibility of change, if change is what's needed.

- Do what is needed in the moment. If you strive for perfection, stop when feedback suggests that this is too exhausting or damaging for your relationships. Accept that there are situations when you need to break your rules, as your rules might keep you away from other people and do not fit what is needed in the situation.

- Accept that you carry your biases and self-deceptions wherever you go—like the rest of us. Your present view of the world is influenced by your past experiences. You don't see the world as it is, but as you are.   .

- Take responsibility for your personal reactions to the world rather than automatically blaming others or expecting the world to change. It means taking responsibility for how you may have contributed to a problem. Do this without harsh self-blame or falling apart.

When you're in flexible mind, you can listen and adapt to other people's needs and feedback, when appropriate, in effective ways. You can adjust to changing circumstances and environments. The social signals that work in the after-work party are different than the signals that work in the office.

So Now You Know

When feeling threatened, you are likely to go to a closed mind-set. There are two opposite poles of the closed mind: a fixed mind and a fatalistic mind. Both block learning from feedback and change, and both negatively impact your relationships. You now know how to recognize if you are in closed mind and what to do when you are, so that you can respond more effectively to others, and find your flexible mind. These steps are summarized in handout 7.1, Loosening the Grip of Fixed Mind, and in handout 7.2, Learning from Fatalistic Mind. We suggest you keep them handy to use from now on. They can help you turn your mind to the possibility of change, live in the moment, and be more flexible.

CHAPTER 8

Shame, Guilt, and Embarrassment (Oh Boy!)

What you're feeling and thinking affects the way you social signal to other people. Shame, guilt, and embarrassment are emotions we all feel and are often the emotions that we have the most difficulty coping with effectively. The way you cope with these emotions can impact your relationships and your willingness to be with other people, and will influence if you're accepted by others or not. Bonds and intimate relationships are built through being vulnerable, open, and showing affection. In this chapter you'll learn about the importance of self-conscious emotions and how to cope with them effectively. Let's take a look.

Belonging to a Group and Self-Conscious Emotions

Long ago, the human species—frail compared to other species, like saber-toothed tigers—survived because humans formed tribes. These tribes were small and nomadic, but they allowed each member to share resources, strengths, and emotional bonds with others. Safety was in numbers. Though physical survival is a lot easier now, humans still need communities. You, me, and the rest of the human race depend on other people for clothes, warmth, food, and other basic needs, including companionship. We are still governed (ruled) by the prehistoric anxious feeling that we are safer if we belong to a group, even just two people. Most people belong to many different communities—family, friendships, work colleagues, religious groups, sports clubs, choirs, an ethnic or cultural group. Just now, you are also a member of a RO DBT community, together with all the people who are reading this book.

Your brain responds to exclusion in the same way it would if you were living in prehistoric times, when belonging to the group gave you best chances for mere survival. In all honesty, if you were living in prehistoric time, rejection by the group would likely have been a death sentence. Thus, you, as all humans, are sensitive to being excluded from community. Your brain is really trying to protect you. You are hardwired to notice signs of social exclusion, and you automatically scan the facial expression of others for signs of disapproval. Are you behaving in an acceptable way? Do they seem to like you? Any facial expression you can't clearly interpret, you'll likely see as disapproving (Davis et al. 2016). And if others disapprove of you, you may feel fearful that they're rejecting you. And this is when emotions such as shame, guilt, and embarrassment can arise. While they may be difficult to experience, they give you important information about your behavior in relationships and can help you protect or repair your connections with others. So activate your social-safety system, and let's take a closer look at some self-conscious emotions. (It's really important.)

Rejection and Self-Conscious Emotions (Ouch!)

So shame, guilt, and embarrassment are often about fearing rejection by others. Rejection by your group hurts! Rejection triggers self-conscious emotions—you doubt that you can remain in the group; you question your position within the group. Though these emotions can give you important information about your behavior, people often desperately try to avoid these emotions, even if they're not aware of their avoidance. To avoid them, you might instantly become angry, withdraw, or lie. Not so helpful for your relationships! So, let's have a closer look at each of these painful emotions.

Shame

You feel shame when you perceive that others disapprove of your real or imagined failings or transgressions to the point that you might be ostracized. You fear or have already experienced public exposure of your violations of social norms or personal faults and weaknesses that damaged the well-being of others. Shame can be a miserable experience (Lynch 2018b).

Disapproval, personal failings, and violations of social norms can be real or imagined. That is, you can feel shame whether shame is warranted or not. Shame is warranted when your personal actions have damaged or ruined others—you took money from your sister's wallet to buy something, caused a car accident because you were texting, embezzled pension funds, and so forth. Let's consider an example from Amy.

When she was a freshman in high school, Amy always dressed differently than her classmates. She encountered stares and felt shame that she was an odd ball out. She sometimes skipped classes to avoid people, but at the same time she felt ashamed for ditching school.

Is Amy's shame warranted or unwarranted? If you said "unwarranted," you're right. Dressing differently than others doesn't harm others. And her unwarranted shame led her to isolate and interfered with several of her valued goals. Let's consider some other examples. Which of the following is warranted shame? (Lynch 2018b)

- Not doing well on a test

- Making something for dinner that didn't taste good

- Not being able to afford what your friends can

- Having an eating disorder

- Having depression

- Bodily functions

In the above examples, no important social norms were broken, and no one was put at risk, harmed, or deceived. In all the above examples, shame is unwarranted.

SIGNALING SHAME WHEN IT'S WARRANTED

It's painful to feel shame. It's the most painful of all the self-conscious emotions. However, the facial expressions, voice, and body language you make when you feel shame will signal to others that you are sorry. Shame triggers you to lower your head, avoid eye contact, and maybe cover your face with your hands. Your slumping shoulders and the shrinking of your whole posture signals your shame. This signals you are submissive, and others are likely to be more sympathetic and less angry when they see this signal. Shame is *pro-social,* as your face, voice, posture, and gestures are signals to others that you want to apologize, appease, and repair your relationship with them. Expressing shame when it's warranted is an important signal to others that you care and that you regret your actions. This can help you regain trust, and you might be forgiven. On the other hand, isolating and withdrawing after warranted shame can damage your relationships, lead to loneliness, and increase behaviors that aren't healthy for you (Lynch 2018b).

HOW TO DEAL WITH SHAME

Use the following skills (Handout 8.1) to deal with warranted shame when you want to repair your relationships with others. Remember that different skills are needed if your shame is unwarranted (see also figure 8.1).

Handout 8.1: Steps to Deal with Shame

1. In the heat of the moment, when feeling ashamed during a social interaction, get into the habit of asking yourself: *What is it that I need to learn from my emotion?* Remember self-enquiry from chapter 4.

2. Ask yourself is your shame warranted. Have you intentionally harmed or deceived another person for personal gain, or has your behavior threatened the well-being of your community? If the answer is yes, your shame is warranted. If the answer is no, your shame is unwarranted.

3. Remember that, most often, people feel unwarranted shame, so carefully consider what kind of shame you are feeling.

4. If your shame is warranted, then *admit it* to yourself, others around you, and especially the person you harmed. If the relationship is important to you, try to repair the relationship without expecting anything in return.

    *   Signal shame by lowering your head, looking down, slumping your shoulders, and shrinking you whole posture. Appear "small."

    *   Take responsibility for your actions with integrity and apologize.

    *   Cheerlead yourself. Remember, people who openly admit warranted shame or guilt are perceived as caring about the well-being of others, and use this to encourage yourself.

    *   If the other person is willing to repair your relationship, combine your apology with cooperative and friendly signals (warm smile, eyebrow wags, eye contact).

5. If shame is *unwarranted,* resist urges to hide, apologize, or appear small and go with opposite behaviors such as:

    *   Behave as if you haven't done anything wrong—because you haven't. However, make sure you check with friends for your blind spots.

    *   Don't apologize.

    *   Signal *confidence.* Stand or sit with your shoulders back and chin up, maintain eye contact. Speak confidently (don't whisper), but stay open to feedback.

Here's a diagram of how to determine whether shame is warranted.

Is Shame Warranted?

- Have I have intentionally harmed or deceived another person for personal gain?

- Did my behavior threaten the well-being of my community?

- Am I the person responsible for the negative consequences of a situation?

If you answered yes to one or more of the above questions, your shame is warranted. If your answers are no, your shame is unwarranted.

Warranted		Unwarranted
If shame is warranted, then **Admit** and try to **Apologize and Appease.**		**Go opposite** to urges to hide or apologize. Behave as if you haven't done anything wrong— because you haven't. Signal confidence.

Figure 8.1

Remember that shame can prevent you from asking for or receiving help. Dealing with shame effectively will help you to learn from feedback, repair your relationships, and get support from others.

PRACTICE OPPORTUNITY!

Think of situations that you feel shame about. Use handout 8.1 to determine if your shame is warranted or not. Then follow through with the steps to deal with warranted shame or unwarranted shame. Practicing helps you be ready to use the skill when a potentially shameful situation happens in the future.

> **Double Extra Special Chill Break**   Wow. We're guessing you've been working hard. It's time to take a break. Call a friend or do something fun. Move around, play a game, listen to music, or take a nap. Tell a joke, or laugh at a comedy routine. Learning about yourself is not a race. We'll wait for you!

Guilt

While shame comes from the way you think others view you and behaviors that significantly harm others, guilt comes from your own negative self-evaluation. When you fail to live according to your own values, you tend to feel guilty. Guilt is an unpleasant emotion, like shame and embarrassment. You may react to the uncomfortable, self-conscious feeling of guilt by bingeing or restricting or punishing yourself through excessive exercise. These strategies of attempting to get rid of uncomfortable feelings aren't effective, can be destructive, and don't rectify the situation or repair relationships. Plus, feeling increasingly guilty or ashamed because of these *behaviors* can set in motion a never-ending cycle of unpleasant emotions. So how do you cope with guilt effectively?

Like shame, guilt can be warranted or unwarranted. The first step in coping with guilt is to determine whether the guilt you're feeling is warranted. How do you know? It's warranted when you've done something wrong, something that wasn't in keeping with your values. For example, if you accidentally dented someone's car and left without leaving a note, guilt would be warranted, as it goes against your value to be an honest person who takes responsibility for your actions. It's unwarranted if you have done nothing wrong or against your values. If someone is sad because you have a ticket to a sold-out play they want to see, feeling guilty that you get to go is unwarranted. In the following examples, check whether you think the guilt is warranted or not warranted:

A. You lie to parents, spouse, or caregivers about important information.

B. You and a friend both apply to the same college. You're accepted, and your friend isn't.

C. You eat dessert.

D. You forgot your mom's birthday and blame your sister for not reminding you.

E. You didn't pass a test, even though you studied.

F. You yell at an employee at the cell phone store.

If you considered A, D, and F to be warranted guilt, we'd agree. People try to avoid their guilty feelings in many different ways. They can signal in unfriendly ways, not take responsibility for our own actions but instead blame others, be unkind to others, and create distrust by lying about important issues, damaging relationships. Those behaviors are against the values that most people hold. Now let's take a look at an example when Suzi becomes aware of her unwarranted guilt.

Suzi's sister, Constance, invited her out for lunch, because she knew Suzi was struggling with isolating, and she wanted to support her. Constance took her to a restaurant famous for chicken tenders. They loved them when they were kids. Suzi recognized the efforts her sister made, so she ate them, even though she hadn't eaten chicken tenders in years. Driving back from the restaurant, Suzi felt overwhelmed with guilt for eating such a high-fat, high-calorie meal. She also knew that if she purged, she'd feel guilty for purging and guilty for lying to her sister (which she'd do if she purged). Realizing that she'd feel guilty no matter what she did, Suzi knew at least some of guilt was unwarranted. She thought about her values, and she realized that lying to her sister was against her value to be honest and that the unwarranted guilt that followed eating chicken tenders was linked with her eating disorder thoughts. This helped Suzi surf the urges to make up for eating those delicious tenders by purging and lying. Then she went opposite the urges to shrink and apologize, as her guilt was unwarranted; instead, she sat up straight in her seat and focused on having a nice evening with her sister in her apartment.

Let's look at your personal experiences. When and in what ways have you behaved in ways that aren't in accordance with your values? (*Alert!* Values are psychologically healthy concepts, not maladaptive beliefs based on eating disordered thinking. Values were discussed in chapter 3, if you want more information. Okay, now back to our topic.) What urges did you have when you violated your values? When you feel guilty, you may have an urge to make amends. You might act on that urge in ways that strengthen relationships, or you may have an urge to hide or attack others because you feel threatened by not living according to your values. Blaming others would be a way of attacking when you feel threatened. Think of times when you have felt guilty. Was the guilt warranted? How did you behave? How did your behavior affect your relationship with the other person?

Situation	Warranted or unwarranted guilt?	What did you signal to others? (facial expression, posture, voice tone, actions)	If warranted, did you take responsibility (without falling apart) and repair what you could?	How did your actions affect your relationship with the other person?

Did you notice any patterns? Do you frequently feel guilty when you haven't done anything wrong? What do you do when you feel guilty?

Guilt is a pro-social emotion (it helps maintain bonds) and is often expressed through apologies and attempts to make amends, such as gifts or acts of service for the other person. It's important to take responsibility and repair the damage you've done to the best of your ability. Interestingly, there's no unique physiological way to express guilt as there is for shame (lowered gaze, hunched shoulders). But at the same time, others tend to distrust expressions of guilt if they *aren't* signaled by the body as shame is. It's the *nonverbal* signals that send the message that you care (Lynch 2018b). Take responsibility, signal with your body that you're sorry, apologize, and repair what you did, if you can. When guilt isn't warranted, remember to go opposite. Going opposite would mean not apologizing or showing a shrinking posture—as in Suzi's example above, sitting up straight in the car. If you are repeatedly apologizing when guilt isn't warranted, others may not trust or believe your apologies when your guilt *is* warranted.

Embarrassment

Minor social transgressions, like loudly farting during the group daily practice of silent meditation, slipping in public, and so on, warrant embarrassment but *not* shame or guilt. Both shame and embarrassment involve similar signals of hanging your head and avoiding eye contact. However, embarrassment also involves smiling, blushing, sometimes nervous face touching (Lynch 2018b). Plus, embarrassment is also more difficult to fake than shame—it's hard to blush on command. Expressing embarrassment is appealing to others. People show embarrassment signals when flirting (coy smiles, blushing). Feeling embarrassed is nothing to be embarrassed about. Feeling embarrassed means that you care about other people, and for this reason they will trust you more. If you show embarrassment, you will be more liked for it. So…

Remember—show embarrassment when embarrassed! When you show embarrassment, others will trust you more, and this will improve your social connections.

So Now You Know

Shame, guilt, and embarrassment are important pro-social emotions. Expressing warranted shame and guilt, along with the confirming social signals, can help you to repair relationships. You have a guide (handout 8.1) to help you recognize if shame and guilt are warranted and how to signal to others your regret. But remember that not all feelings of shame and guilt are warranted. When shame and guilt are unwarranted, stay confident and go opposite. Then there's embarrassment. Expressing embarrassment will make you more likeable and trusted, so go ahead, no reason to feel embarrassed about your embarrassment—show it!

CHAPTER 9

Social Comparisons, Envy, Bitterness, and Harsh Judgments (Oh My!)

So far, we've focused on adjusting your social signaling to increase connections with others. But that's only one part of relationships. Another part is learning to approach others with openness and authenticity about your thoughts and feelings to build the kind of trust that helps you form friendships and feel part of a community. In this chapter, we'll practice behaviors that cultivate openness, trust, and deepen connection with others.

When you're an individual with overcontrolled coping, being open with your thoughts and feelings, new ideas, and the feedback of others most likely is not what you learned as you grew up nor is it your natural inclination. You're more likely to adhere to the "never let them see you sweat" school of thought and have armor to cover up the emotions that make you vulnerable in social situations (see chapter 6). Whether you put on your armor is likely influenced by your internal experiences: thoughts, urges, emotions, and sensations. Some of these experiences are particularly characteristic of OC coping, like social comparisons, envy, and bitterness. If you often compare yourself with others and envy others, you're likely to harshly judge yourself and others and to be bitter about past experiences. You likely don't want others to know about your envy, judgments, or bitterness, so you put on a mask to hide it.

Social comparisons, envy, bitterness, and harsh judgments affect your social signaling and can interfere with relationships. It's difficult to signal openness and friendliness when you're stewing bitterly behind your mask. So here we'll look at social comparisons and some ways to cope. We'll also discuss increasing social connections both through forgiveness (of others or yourself) for behaviors that might otherwise lead to anger, resentment, or self-blame, and through grieving the disappointments we might encounter in life—the loss we feel when we realize some aspect of life isn't as we want it to be. So get something to drink, take a deep breath, lean back, and we'll start with social comparisons.

Social Comparisons with Envy

Social comparison is a natural, inborn drive to evaluate yourself in comparison to others. Making social comparisons is normal—we all do it. Comparing yourself to others (their clothes, grades, academic degrees, best marathon time, all their volunteer work, their hundreds of social media likes) is a measure of where you stand in the various groups you belong to. Comparing yourself to others can give you important information, like what you want to pursue for yourself. If you envy someone's birthday celebrations with friends, that's clearly something you want. So you could work on developing that for yourself. But envy can be a problem if the comparison with another doesn't lead to, say, planning a birthday party for yourself. Maybe you often use social comparisons to determine your worth as a person, sometimes thinking you're better than others and sometimes that you're inferior. That roller coaster (*I'm the best! No, I'm the worst!*) can make you dizzy, anxious, and confused about your self-worth. Plus, when you use social comparisons to determine your worth, winning can become all-important. You may lie or cheat or act in self-destructive ways to get ahead—to win—even when winning doesn't matter in the big picture. You may show contempt toward someone who achieved something you don't think they deserved, pout or go silent when you don't get your way, and engage in gossip and sarcasm to put others down. You may refuse to help others (why give away your advantage?) and secretly smile when a rival suffers. Yikes. Not exactly a way to build a community! What do you think—does this describe you sometimes?

Envy results when you compare yourself to someone and decide that they have it better than you. You want what they have, whether it's something about their appearance, achievements, lifestyle, social connections, or personality. It's also likely that you see it as unfair that they have it and you don't.

Envy can be helpful or unhelpful (Lynch 2018b). Helpful envy is like admiring what someone has achieved, like envying someone's success in journalism that clarifies your own goals and motivates you in your own work, your own career. It can help you determine what you value and to get going on it. Ah, but then there's unhelpful envy. That's another story.

Unhelpful Envy

Unhelpful envy is when you want what's unrealistic and unattainable, like bodies or lifestyles. Social media can show people as having perfect lives, but humans aren't perfect and can't have perfect lives. Unhelpful envy can also make you focus on the unfairness of someone having what you want. You want to ball up your fists and shout, "It's not fair! It's just not fair!" And maybe you want to hide your feelings and perhaps hide away yourself.

Unhelpful envy includes a combination of shame and anger. The anger may come about as a result of the shame: "I hate you because when I compare myself to you I feel ashamed." When this happens, thoughts of revenge are often quick to follow. You want the envied person to hurt. You want to get even, though you know that's not okay. As people tend to frown on revenge thinking, you keep your thoughts secret.

Revenge can be impulsive—acting without thinking and throwing someone's phone in the pool. It can also be carefully planned—posting private information online, secretly switching out someone's food for something they don't eat, baking someone something high in calories when you think they are thinner than you. You may want to get back at the person and show them that they're not all that great. See how John shares his experiences with unhelpful envy:

I'm always comparing myself to other runners. I compare my lean body mass to those I train with. I check with other runners about their carb intake. I track my best times, as well those of others. When mine are better, I feel proud—even a bit arrogant, if I'm honest. If I don't come in first in my age group, I judge myself as a "loser" and envy the person who won. Especially Eric. It's really not fair. Eric grew up in a family who supported his training, and they still do. He has the money to hire a coach. He's single and doesn't even have to work full-time, so he has lots of time to train. When I see him ahead of me in a race, I hope he'll trip or something. He wins a lot, and all these people swarm around him and congratulate him like he's some kind of king. Someday I'll show him he's not so great.

Have you experienced social comparisons and unhelpful envy? Here's a hint. If you see someone as a rival, you're likely to be feeling unhelpful envy. The first step in coping with unhelpful envy is to be aware that's what you're feeling.

Coping with Unhelpful Envy

Unhelpful envy can be destructive. When you're focused on unfairness and revenge, you're not bulding your own life or contributing to or connecting with others. What to do? To cope with unhelpful envy, the first step is to determine if you're experiencing unhelpful envy. The following worksheet will help (Lynch 2018b, 479).

Worksheet 9.1: Are You Experiencing Unhelpful Envy?

Write yes or no next to each question.

	Do you feel that you have been wronged, neglected, or passed over by this person or others?
	Do you find yourself thinking negative thoughts about this person or group?
	Do you find yourself gossiping about this person frequently?
	Have you fantasized about getting back at them?
	Have you tried to make their life difficult?
	Do you desire to punish them, beat them, or prove them wrong?
	Do you find yourself enjoying any misfortune that befalls them or fantasizing about misfortune occurring?
	Do you seek agreement from others that the person deserves to be punished or has an unfair advantage?

John answered yes to many of those questions. If you did too, the next step is to admit that you're envious. Yeah, that's not always easy to do. You might find yourself saying, "I'm not envious. The whole situation is just unfair." Sound familiar? And maybe someone like Eric *does* have an unfair advantage. But the point is, are you experiencing envy? And is that envy destructive? If you are experiencing unhelpful envy, it's important to admit it to yourself. It's kind of difficult to change something if you don't think you have it!

Now that you're aware of unhelpful envy, identify the thoughts and urges that go along with that emotion—thoughts and urges that can lead you to behave in ways that leave you more isolated and disconnected. Knowing these thoughts and urges helps you to cope with the emotion. Here's a list of actions and urges that tend to come from envy.

Worksheet 9.2: Actions and Urges from Envy
Adapted from Lynch (2018b)

Think of someone you consider a rival; answer yes or no to each question.

	Do you have urges for revenge, to get even or make the envied person's life difficult?
	Do you behave coldly toward them?
	Do you talk to them or about them in a sarcastic tone?
	Do you deny your feelings about them?
	Do you keep your feelings secret?
	Do you hide from or avoid them?
	Do you gossip about them and seek confirmation?
	Do you avoid using the word "envy" to hide your feelings and to keep your desires for revenge secret?
	Do you take pleasure in their failings?

If you answered yes to one or more, do these behaviors fit with your values and your valued goals? Probably not, we're guessing. Okay, then do you want to change your unhelpful envy? Hold on. Give this some thought. Think of some times when you felt this envy. Perhaps you are right now? Now, thinking about specific situations in which you've felt it, what are the reasons you would want to give it up?

_____

_____

_____

If you're ready to work on unhelpful envy, let's get going. One option is to change unhelpful envy into helpful envy—look at what you envy and use that information to make plans for your own life. If you envy a friend's job working with children, how could you create a similar experience for yourself?

Another strategy is to go opposite. You've already learned this skill in chapter 7, so now we can look at how to apply it here. To go opposite, first determine which type of unhelpful envy you're experiencing: unhelpful envious anger and unhelpful shameful envy. With envious anger, your urges are to hurt the other person. There are several ways to experience envious anger, thus different ways to go opposite.

Worksheet 9.3: Going Opposite to Envious Anger

Adapted from Lynch (2018b)

Going Opposite To	A General Idea for Going Opposite	Examples for Going Opposite	What You Will Do
Imagining ways to get revenge	Block those thoughts	Consider and list reasons the other person may deserve their good fortune; focus on gratitude for what you have or on actions you are taking for your own betterment	
Behaving coldly	Practice kindness	Speak kindly, do kind actions, be honest	
Talking about them with a sarcastic tone	Stop harsh judgments	Recognize that you may be wrong in your thoughts; give yourself something else to think about; out yourself to someone you trust and ask for help	
Denying feelings about the person	Acknowledge feelings	Be honest with yourself; use self-enquiry to see what you can learn	
Hiding from or avoiding the person	Stop hiding	Go about your normal activities; go to events without checking to see if the envied person will be there	
Fantasizing about them failing	Block those fantasies	Practice self-enquiry about what you need to learn; activate social safety before interacting with the envied person	

Blocking means to stop unwanted thoughts. Thus the first step is to be sure you *want* to stop them. They can feel good in the moment! If you are sure that you want to stop, focus on the envious thoughts. Then shout (or think) "Stop!" and replace the thought with a more positive thought. It's normal for the thoughts to recur. It will take time for them to stop entirely. Once you are able to stop the thoughts, then you can practice saying stop in a normal voice tone, and then perhaps a whisper.

Now let's look at how to go opposite to unhelpful, shameful envy.

Worksheet 9.4: Going Opposite to Unhelpful Shameful Envy

Adapted from Lynch (2018b)

Going Opposite To	A General Idea for Going Opposite	Examples for Going Opposite	What You Will Do
Giving up your values in this situation	Live your values	Write your values that apply in this situation, how you would behave if you were living according to your values?	
Denying your envy	Admit your envy	Label your emotions with no justifications, rationalizations, or blaming; be clear about what you are envious about and assess whether you truly want what the other person has.	
Hiding your envy	Reveal your envy to an objective, caring person	Tell a caring person who will be truthful with you; use the word, "envy" and let them know you want to change.	
Wishing the envied person would fail, negative actions toward person	Wish the person success	Celebrate the successes of the person; focus on what you admire and want to develop for yourself. If you want a relationship, apologize for any past behaviors that caused harm and out yourself to the person about your envy.	

Here's an example from John:

To deal with the envy he felt for Eric, John met with Eric in a private place. He then shared with Eric, "I just wanted to let you know that I have been so envious of your successes and all the support that you have for your running, that I started to wish that bad things would happen to you. I was feeling angry toward you, and I know I've been cold toward you and sometimes critical. I apologize for my thoughts and actions that came from my envy. I realize that I admire what you've done."

Now it's your turn. Think of a situation where you experienced unhelpful envy. Was it envious anger or shameful envy? If envious anger, complete worksheet 9.3, writing how you will go opposite to the behaviors you're experiencing. For practicing kindness (going opposite to behaving coldly), if you no longer see the envied person, use visualization to practice being kind to the person. Really picture that person clearly and see yourself being supportive and friendly. If you're thinking of an experience of shameful envy, complete worksheet 9.4. Push yourself to do each step fully and to go completely opposite from unhelpful envy behaviors. And, hey, don't skip the step about revealing your envy to someone who is a caring, objective person. 😊

As mentioned before, just reading this information, while it's helpful for understanding, is unlikely to make any difference in your life. It's important to practice the steps we've just talked about.

It's also important to understand that envy is likely to recur. That's normal. Whenever you experience unhelpful envy, go through the worksheets again so it doesn't block your relationships with others. Practice going opposite again and again, whenever unhelpful envy shows up.

CHILLLLLLLLL Break!   Good work! Now relax for a moment ... or two. Or a few. Or more. Take a deep breath. This chapter is part of the "leaning in" part of RO DBT, meaning that you don't push away difficult thoughts, urges, and emotions—you consider what you can learn from them. You may experience unpleasant sensations while working on these topics. Don't push them away or skip a difficult exercise. Really consider the questions and options as you go through this material. Lean back, relax. What are you learning about yourself in this chapter? Perhaps you might consider a self-enquiry question (chapter 4)? When you're ready, we'll talk about bitterness.

Bitterness

Welcome back! When you believe that other people are to blame when you've failed to reach important goals or didn't get what you saw as rightfully yours, you may experience bitterness. While envy is an emotion that comes and goes, bitterness can last for long periods of time. Bitterness can influence all parts of your life. When you're bitter, you tend to be pessimistic, discouraged, and resentful. You hold grudges and probably believe that happiness is impossible. Are you experiencing bitterness? If so, it's likely to make you unhappy and discontent and keep you from having close relationships.

But first you have to identify bitterness. The following worksheet should help (Lynch 2018b, 498).

Worksheet 9.5: Are You Experiencing Bitterness?
Adapted from Lynch (2018b)

Answer yes or no to the following questions.

	Do you find it difficult to accept help from others (or give help)?
	Do people close to you think that you hold a grudge too long? Is there a past injury that you cannot let go of?
	Do you find it difficult to give compliments to others (or receive them)?
	Do you feel that your efforts often go unrecognized?
	Do you find yourself ruminating when people don't appreciate what you have done?
	Do you sometimes tell yourself that trying to get what you want is just not possible?
	Do you feel resigned to your fate or say to yourself, "Why bother?"
	Do you feel that enthusiasm about life is misguided or naïve?
	Are you a cynic?
	Do you feel that you have not achieved what you should have in life?
	Do you feel that life has treated you unfairly and that this happens most of the time?
	Do you frequently find yourself questioning the intentions of others?
	Do you frequently find yourself believing that others judge you or are out to cause you harm?

If you answered yes to most of those questions, guess what? Yeah, bitterness. If you are experiencing bitterness, are you willing to let it go? The following exercise will help you decide if you really want to let go of it. If you don't, opposite action will not work.

Letting Go of Bitterness

Think of a particular person (or a group) that you feel bitterness toward, and answer the questions as honestly as possible.

What are the pros and cons of having bitterness toward them? List them.

Pros:

_____

_____

_____

Cons:

_____

_____

_____

Would you like to have a better relationship with them? (Circle one: yes or no)

What are your values in this situation? Are you behaving according to your values?

_____

_____

_____

Remind yourself of times in the past when winning or being right did not work well in terms of living your values or in terms of relationships with others. What happened?

_____

_____

_____

Remember times when you achieved goals only to discover that their importance faded over time.

_____

_____

_____

Do you truly desire the advantage that you see the other person having? If you do truly desire the advantage, is there a way that you can achieve it, rather than being locked in the bitterness you feel right now?

_____

_____

_____

Okay, if you're ready to let go of bitterness, let's move on to the next step.

Actions and Urges from Bitterness

To let go of bitterness, you again use the skill of going opposite. (Going opposite of unhelpful emotions can be really helpful in many situations!) To go opposite, of course, you have to know what actions and urges come from bitterness, so let's identify them. Here are some actions and urges to watch for. Check off the ones that apply to you.

☐ Are you being judgmental toward hopeful, optimistic, or enthusiastic people and experiences?

☐ Are you preventing or minimizing expressions of happiness?

☐ Are you spending time brooding?

☐   Do you reject help from others?

☐   Are you experiencing pleasure when others suffer misfortune?

☐   Do you consider progress impossible or naïve?

☐   Do you find it difficult to give compliments or receive them?

☐   Do you typically listen or seek out negative, cynical stories and entertainment?

Coping with Bitterness

Once you know the urges and actions you want to target, it's time to practice going opposite to them. Consider the characteristics of bitterness in the chart below and write how you will practice going opposite.

Worksheet 9.6: Go Opposite to Bitterness

Go opposite to	How will you practice going opposite?
Preventing and minimizing expressions of happiness	
Brooding	
Rejecting help	
Negatively judging people who are happy or hopeful	
Expressing or enjoying pleasure when others suffer	
Not giving or rejecting compliments	
Seeking out negative entertainment or information	
Expressing expectations of negative outcomes or hopelessness	

For example, you might practice giving compliments or accepting them and reading some books that are optimistic and have happy endings. Going opposite to bitterness means increasing your sense of compassion for others. So practice being compassionate. Listen to news stories about people making a positive difference in the world. Or focus on what you have in common with your fellow human beings—every day, with your social-safety system activated, repeat the following script to yourself (Lynch 2018b, 492).

Commonalities Script

Just like me, others are seeking happiness and have known suffering. Just like me, they have harmed others and have been harmed by others. Just like me, they are trying to cope with their lives as best they can and yet are still learning.

- Activate your social-safety system (see chapter 5). Then interact with individuals who have different ways of dressing, thinking, or acting than you.

- Activate your social-safety system. Then listen to the opinions of people who hold different values or morals than you.

Tracking your practice on the following worksheet will help you make changes. (You can also download this worksheet at https://www.newharbinger.com/48930.)

Worksheet 9.7: Increasing Compassion for Others Practice

Write yes or no for each practice. Keep track of your activities for a week.

Day	Repeated commonalities script	Focused on news about altruism	Interacted with others who think differently than me, with openness	Interacted with people who dress and act differently than I do, with openness	Kindly asked someone with a different view to explain their thinking
M					
T					
W					
Th					
F					
S					
S					

When you let go of bitterness and increase your compassion for others, you open up opportunities to connect and live your values. Social comparisons, envy, and bitterness are often related to harsh judgments of yourself, others, or both. Those judgments can impact your social signals to others.

Harsh Judgments

Like envy, judging is something that humans do. We judge all the time. Judging is not good or bad in itself. The problem is often not about the judgment, but what happens as a result of the judgment. Judging others can lead to rumination and brooding, make you less open to feedback and new information, keep you in your threat system, and negatively impact how you socially signal or express your intentions and experience to others (Lynch 2018b). Ultimately, when you judge others or yourself, it leads you to patterns of behavior that can block creating connections with others. Yikes!

One of the problems with harsh judgments is that you can view them as facts. You judge someone as generally "boring" or "cruel," and you tend believe the judgment without learning anything else about them or the circumstances. Someone cuts you off on the freeway, and you might call them "reckless" only to learn that they were trying to get to a hospital. This tendency to take your own judgments for reality can be true in more everyday situations as well. Here's an example. Imagine that you meet John at an evening get-together. He doesn't make eye contact, has little to say, and seems tense. You assume he thinks he's better than you, but actually he's worried about getting home—ten miles on the schedule tomorrow morning! Had you met him another time, you might have enjoyed his sense of humor and his interest in classic movies and spy novels. But you've judged him as someone you don't want to get to know, so when you see him again, you avoid him and are aloof and distant with him.

Judgments can also lead to rumination and can impact how you social signal or express yourself to others (Lynch 2018b). Imagine that your friend is talking about her vacation, but you are in your head thinking how spoiled she is (judgment of her), how expensive her trip was, and how you're a loser since you can't afford a trip like that (judgment of self), or how much more exciting her trip was than any place you've been. You move into your threat system (see chapter 5). You wish you could go on trips like that (envy). You decide she thinks she's better than you (judgment), and you want to get back at her. Why should she have such great trips? You feel an urge to sabotage her next trip, while putting on a mask to hide your emotions. And it all started with judging her as spoiled because she was talking about her trip. See how this can impact your social signaling with this person—and maybe others too? If you're thinking how arrogant someone is, you're probably not showing friendly social signals. You may signal that you aren't interested, or you may have a flat or nonexpressive face (signaling anger), or you might put on a fake smile that the other person sees through. Pouting, gossip, shutting conversation down and walking away, and phony smiling—all are signals that may come from harsh judgments, and all are ways of shutting down and being unavailable to connect.

Judging others and fantasizing about revenge and misfortune are some of the reasons that many individuals with OC inwardly believe that they are not very nice people. They can also harbor harsh *self-judgments* as a result of their past mistakes, incidents of expressing intense emotions when they didn't intend to do so, or hurtful acts directed toward others. Could that be true for you? If so, keep in mind that taking responsibility is different from judging yourself harshly. In fact, harsh judgments may be a way of avoiding true responsibility. Ruminating about how awful you are doesn't repair relationships or change future behavior and likely leads to you withdrawing (and not contributing) to those you love.

Coping with Harsh Judgments

The first step in coping effectively with judgments so they don't block your connections with others is simple awareness of them. You may judge harshly without awareness you are doing so. To increase your awareness, notice times when your body is tense. That's often a cue that there's a harsh judgment present (Lynch 2018b).

Use the chart below (and available at https://www.newharbinger.com/48930) to help increase your awareness of your body tension, judgments, social signaling, and whether your behavior is fitting with your values or not. When you notice your body is tense, look for hidden judgments. Then notice your social signaling. What is your facial expression? Are you withdrawing from the conversation? Does your social signal move you closer to your valued goals or further away?

Worksheet 9.8: Coping with Harsh Judgments

Date	Event	Body Tension (1 to 5)	Harsh Judgment	Social signaling	Does social signaling fit with your values?

Once you're aware of harsh judgments, there are strategies that help you cope with them. Some you can use the moment a judgment arises, such as activating social safety, engaging flexible mind, practicing the mindfulness exercise known as the "awareness continuum," and in-the-moment self-enquiry. Other strategies are longer term, like self-enquiry, giving the benefit of the doubt, allowing grief, and forgiveness (Lynch 2018b).

1. ACTIVATE SOCIAL SAFETY

When you notice tension in your body and identify a harsh judgment, one of the first things you can do—the moment you notice the judgment—is to activate your social-safety system (see chapter 5). Activating social safety will decrease the judgment's hold on you and will also help you change your social signaling and be better able to connect.

2. ENGAGE FLEXIBLE MIND

In the situation where you are experiencing harsh judgments, are you operating from fixed mind or fatalistic mind? If you are, follow the suggestions in chapter 7 to let go of or lessen the intensity of harsh judgments that are coming from those mind states. When you work on addressing the harsh judgments that come from fixed and fatalistic mind, you can begin to activate flexible mind in the moment, right when you are having the harsh judgment.

3. AWARENESS CONTINUUM

The awareness continuum is a mindfulness exercise in RO DBT that helps you be open about your internal experiences and learn to distinguish between thoughts, emotions, sensations, and images (Lynch 2018b, 260–61). It is a way to step off the path of blaming others or yourself. When you practice the awareness continuum, you are creating awareness that your thoughts are just thoughts, not necessarily reality. You're also taking responsibility for your judgments by labeling them. The idea is to notice your judgments so you don't automatically accept them as truth.

How do you practice the awareness continuum?

1. Start by saying the word "I."

2. Clarify that you are mindfully observing by adding the words "am aware of."

3. Label what is being observed by classifying it as one of your different forms: sensation, emotion, image, or thought. Sensations are any experience involving taste, sound, touch, smell, or sight. Emotions include emotional experiences and mood states, urges, impulses, and desires. Images generally fall into observations about the past (such as a memory) or imagining what others might be thinking or feeling.

4. Describe the content of the experience without explanation, rationalization, or justification. Don't give any whys. And don't clump ideas together. Clumping means that you combine different categories in the same sentence. Describe being aware of only one sensation, thought, or one emotion in a sentence. Only one!

Here's an example of Antonio practicing the awareness continuum exercise when he becomes aware of harsh judgments toward a friend named Joe:

"I am aware of tension in my jaw."

"I am aware of tightness in my chest."

"I am aware of the thought that Joe's arms are more muscular than mine."

"I am aware of the thought that Joe thinks I look ridiculous."

"I am aware of a feeling of fear."

"I am aware of the thought that I am not good enough."

"I am aware of the emotion of shame."

"I am aware of a queasy sensation in my stomach."

"I am aware of the image of being made fun of as a child."

"I am aware of the urge to work even harder to develop my physique."

It's so easy to accept thoughts as facts and feelings as truth. The awareness continuum can help you be more aware of your thoughts, emotions, and the truth of the adage, "just because your think it doesn't mean it's true." Also, having an emotion doesn't mean that feeling is someone else's responsibility. If you're feeling envy, for example, it's important to be aware of the feeling, then decide what (if any) action should be taken, rather than harshly judging the other person for the envy that you yourself feel.

Take a moment and practice the awareness continuum now. This is a private exercise, just for you—it's not done in front of others. It can be done aloud or silently. Remember to start with "I am aware of ..." and then just say one thing. Practice for a minute.

Practice the awareness continuum on a regular basis, when you're walking or driving or washing the dishes. Let it be something that flows for you. You want to practice it *before* you're in a difficult situation, so when you do notice tension or are aware of a harsh judgment, you'll be at ease with the awareness continuum.

4. SELF-ENQUIRY

Once you notice your judgmental thoughts, another option for coping with them is to use self-enquiry to learn more about your responses. You can use self-enquiry in the moment or after the fact. Follow the steps for self-enquiry in chapter 4 to examine your edges around harsh judgments. To use self-enquiry in the moment, notice that you are having harsh judgments, then ask yourself, "What is there for me to learn about myself from my having these harsh judgments now?"

5. GIVING THE BENEFIT OF THE DOUBT

When we make assumptions and judgments about other people, they're usually negative. It's not so often that we assume the best about others: "John must have had a good reason for not showing up for my dinner." No. The other person is guilty until proven innocent. This makes sense in terms of how we evolved. It's better to mistake a bush as a tiger than a tiger as a bush! But today, in your everyday interactions with others, you are better served by making neutral or benign interpretations. So when you notice that you've made a harsh judgment, notice that you are assuming the worst and consider other options that are valid and reasonable. Then consider giving the other person the benefit of the doubt. For example, imagine that your boss, in a neutral, matter-of-fact tone, says, "Didn't you say you would be here early today?" The harsh judgment could be, "She's mad that I didn't come in early. She is so critical. She is the worst boss in the company." When you notice the harsh judgment, ask yourself what other interpretations are possible?

- She is confused and looking for clarification.

- She is wondering if everything is okay.

- She is just confirming that you made the statement.

- She is concerned that something went wrong and delayed you.

- She is just making conversation.

Notice too that if you have a strong reaction to what your boss said, it is a good self-enquiry opportunity to learn more about yourself (see chapter 4).

6. GRIEVING YOUR DISAPPOINTMENTS

Harsh judgments are often about disappointment—how you wish something were, how you wanted it to be, how you think it should be, letting someone down, or someone letting you down. Harsh judgments can be about the loss of something or someone.

Antonio remembers feeling upset when his sister said that if he would just eat normally instead of bingeing all night, his problems would be over. She often said that she thought he just wanted attention and didn't want to grow up. He was hurt and angry that she still, after many years, didn't understand his eating disorder. If she loved him, she would be supportive! And why did she have to make cookies all the time? She was just cold and mean and trying to control him. But then again, he thought, she's probably right. I'm so flawed and broken that I couldn't even keep a job or stick to an eating plan.

By talking with his therapist, Antonio realized that behind his judgments was disappointment. He felt let down by his sister. He wanted a sister who would support him in his recovery, and he didn't have that. If you have this experience of a friend or loved one judging you when you want them to be supportive, you'll likely have a lot of emotions. Harsh judgments can get in the way of being aware of these emotions and coping effectively. You can release harsh judgments by grieving your losses. Maybe you judge your sister for not being more supportive. The loss is that you wanted a sister who would be there for you (or would visit you more or something else). To grieve a loss like this, identify your harsh judgment. What were your expectations (of yourself or others) that were not met? For Antonio, his loss was that he didn't have a sister who would learn about his disorder to understand it, validate him about how difficult recovery was, and be kind (and honest) when he didn't follow through. He also felt a loss of hope that he'd be able to stick to his nutrition plan and not slip back into his eating disorder.

In the space below, write about a loss that you experienced when your expectations weren't met. Don't choose your biggest loss for now.

_____

_____

_____

Now repeat the script below three times in a row for several days or weeks, until you feel yourself letting go of the harsh judgment (Lynch 2018b, 314).

I am learning to face the pain of my loss of expectations or beliefs about how things should or ought to be when events don't go as planned or when other people don't behave as expected, without getting down on myself, falling apart, or automatically blaming others. I am learning to recognize that my harsh judgments often stem from a desire to avoid self-examination, avoid taking responsibility, or avoid accepting that I cannot control the world. For today's practice, I need to grieve the loss of my expectations that [insert your particular expectations here]. My sadness helps me recognize that the world is not always as I expect it to be. By allowing myself to experience the sadness of this loss, I am learning to let go of my unhelpful judgments.

7. FORGIVENESS

Finally, a way to cope with harsh judgments is to practice forgiveness of others and of yourself. Forgiveness does not mean that you approve of what happened or that you are forgetting it. It doesn't mean opening yourself up to hurt again. It means taking care of yourself and letting go of useless anger, resentment, or self-blame. It's about adjusting to circumstances in an ever-changing world for your own well-being and those you love.

Think of someone that you are holding a grudge against. Got it? Now practice forgiveness by using the HEART skill (Lynch 2018b, 506).

- Identify the past *Hurt*.

- Locate your *Edge* that's keeping you stuck in the past.

- *Acknowledge* that forgiveness is a choice.

- *Reclaim* your life by grieving your loss and practicing forgiveness.

- Practice *Thankfulness* and then pass it on.

Let's go through the process step by step.

- Identify the past *Hurt*. What is it that you need to forgive yourself or others for?

- Locate your *Edge* that's keeping you stuck in the past. Remember that your *edge* in RO DBT is your psychological unknown. It refers to actions, sensations, feelings, thoughts, and images that you want to avoid, that you feel embarrassed about, or that you prefer not to admit to others (Lynch, 2018b).

- *Acknowledge* that forgiveness is a choice. Once you know what the hurt is and what your energy is about, recognize that forgiveness is your choice. You don't have to forgive. It's really for you. You're most likely the one who is suffering as a result of not forgiving, and you're the one living with difficult emotions about the situation. It's likely that the only life that would be changed is yours. Deciding to forgive is reclaiming your life. If you decide to forgive, practice the following script for forgiving and reclaiming your life.

- *Reclaim* Your Life. When you are ready, repeat the following script.

I recognize that to forgive and reclaim my life, I must first grieve my loss of my expectations or beliefs about the world, myself, or other people. For today's practice, I need to grieve the loss of my expectations that [insert your particular expectations here]. By grieving this loss, I am learning to recognize that I cannot avoid the pain of this past injury—it is not something that I can ignore, deny, or pretend never happened—as this only creates more suffering. My sadness helps me recognize that the world is not always as I expect it to be. By allowing myself to experience the sadness of my loss—without getting down on myself, falling apart, or blaming others—I take the first step toward forgiveness and genuine healing. I recognize that forgiveness is freely chosen. And so, with full awareness, I freely choose to forgive.

Turn your mind to the area in your life needing forgiveness. Take a slow, deep breath, raise your eyebrows, smile a closed-mouth smile, and say:

I forgive you [deep breath]. I forgive you [deep breath]. I forgive you [deep breath]. I recognize that this brief practice of forgiveness means taking care of myself, and that by repeating this practice frequently, I am freeing myself from useless anger, resentment, or rumination and reclaiming my life by taking a step toward living more fully in the present.

- Practice *Thankfulness* and then pass it on. After you've done the script, be thankful for what you have. Remind yourself of all the times in your life when you have needed forgiveness from others and be thankful that you can offer forgiveness to others.

Practice forgiveness over and over, whenever harsh judgments related to grudges arise. Remember, it's for you and your mental well-being.

Now You Know ...

Social signaling matters! Your thoughts and emotions can affect your social signals and thus impact your relationships. There are internal experiences that OC people are particularly likely to have, like envy or bitterness, that affect your social signaling and can keep you from building satisfying and nourishing connections with others. Harsh judgments of yourself and others can do the same. Being able to forgive others and yourself and to grieve the loss of your expectations of others and yourself is important in maintaining positive connections with others. The skills you are learning are life skills to use on an ongoing basis. And oh, by the way, are you practicing self-enquiry?

Are You with Us?

You've learned so much at this point, and *of course* you are practicing what you are learning so it makes a difference in your life. You know your valued goals, which can guide you in making decisions (chapter 3). You're practicing radical openness and self-enquiry (chapter 4). You know the importance of activating your social-safety system and how to do it in social interactions (chapter 5). You've identified the ways you socially signal that might block connections with others and skills to use to be more open (chapter 6). And you know how to cope with unhelpful envy, bitterness, and harsh judgments. If you don't remember or aren't practicing any of these tools, this would be a good time to go back, review, and find ways to practice what you have learned. Finally, be sure to recognize the positive changes you have made!

CHAPTER 10

Social Engagement: We Aren't Talking Marriage, Just Connection (Whoops! We Don't Want to Scare You!)

Have you ever felt totally alone in a room full of friends? This can happen due to low social engagement—the degree to which you participate in a community, society, or group. How do you interact with those around you? With your friends? Family? Are you the sort who hangs on the sidelines? In this chapter you will come to understand how you may avoid connecting with others, intentionally or not. After all, you have to show up to build connection. There are three ways we often block or avoid connection: going absent, lying, and with indirect communication. You'll learn what indirect social signaling is and how it can contribute to fewer true connections. In addition, we'll discuss how indirect social signaling, including "pushbacks" and "don't hurt me's," push people farther away. We'll review skills that can help you put your values above your secret desires for control. Finally, we'll discuss the ROCKs ON skill to enhance kindness and social connections with others (Lynch 2018b, 355–56).

Going Absent (Ghosting)

While connection is crucial to our well-being, it isn't always easy. We have to be vulnerable and signal in ways that help us connect, but that can feel scary and unnatural. We may not even be aware of things we do that may interfere with making friends and deepening relationships. And worrying about what to say or how to respond in the "right" way can make us so nervous that we do it "wrong,"—or we don't respond at all, something called "ghosting." The effort needed to connect can seem too much. We might give up. Have you ever thought, *I cannot be bothered,* and turned down an opportunity to be social? But how often can you turn down invitations before the invitations stop? Remember the aloof and distant style of relating?

Perhaps you are the person who goes to a party because you were invited. It's the right thing to do, to show up. Seventy-five minutes into the party, people start asking where you went. They can't find you, because you slipped out the back when no one was looking. After all, you stayed the prescribed hour and fifteen minutes. ☺ You certainly wouldn't say goodbye to anyone—they might try to talk you into staying! What might your behavior signal to people at the party? Do you struggle to return phone calls or respond to texts? Have you noticed that the longer you delay, the harder it gets to respond? Then maybe you don't respond at all? What might that signal to others? They might think you don't value the relationship? Putting in effort to connect can be tiring, and it can feel like a risk of rejection or boredom or social discomfort. But having no connection at all typically leads to depression.

Suzi and her friend Aliyah talked regularly, at least every two weeks. But when Suzi was in intensive treatment, she didn't return Aliyah's call for over three weeks. She didn't want to explain how much she was struggling. She didn't think about how this might make Aliyah feel, what it signaled to her. Finally, Aliyah texted her, "I miss you, Suzi. I'd love to catch up!" Suzi missed Aliyah too, so she texted that she would call that night. Aliyah responded, "Great! Any time!"

Later that afternoon, Suzi had a difficult talk with her sister, Constance. Suzi cried a bit, and although the conversation ended well, she was exhausted. She wanted to talk with Aliyah, but she felt overwhelmed. She thought, "The best thing to do would be to go to bed, pull up the covers, and watch TV. After all, isn't practicing being kind to myself what I'm supposed to be working on?" (Do you hear the justification she's giving herself?)

The next day Suzi felt guilty for not calling Aliyah, but she felt she would have to explain why—and explain why she hadn't called at all in the last month—and the thought of that conversation was too much: "I don't know what to say or how to say it. And now maybe she's upset with me. I can't deal with this." So she continued to avoid calling her, and every time she thought of it, the pangs of guilt and fear got worse.

Finally Constance asked her what was bothering her, and she explained it. Constance helped her realize that by avoiding the short-term discomfort of self-disclosure, vulnerability, and emotional energy, she was creating long-term discomfort and stress. She felt guilty, worried she had damaged a friendship she valued, and was preoccupied with the inevitable conversation hanging over her head. She might even lose Aliyah as a friend. Suzi and Constance discussed what she could do in the future instead of just ghosting. [You know patterns have a way of repeating themselves, ☺.] They came up with several options. She could have called Aliyah and told her honestly that she had had a rough conversation earlier and wasn't up to talking. She could have texted and set up another time to talk. Or maybe she could have texted and, lying, said that something had come up and that she was unable to call. All these options would have gone opposite to her urge to withdraw.

What would you do?

Worksheet 10.1: Invisible or Not-So-Invisible Ghosting

Think of a time in the last two weeks when you had the urge to not respond, to leave, to not reach out, or other ways of ghosting someone. Describe the situation:

_____

_____

_____

_____

_____

What was your action urge? What did you want to do?

_____

_____

_____

_____

What would be the action that is opposite to your urge?

_____

_____

_____

_____

_____

So go do it, already!

While not ghosting might seem passive, it is still a significant social signal. Perhaps you think, *Eh, no one will even notice.* (Come on, do you actually believe that? ☺) Not responding and not showing up are powerful signals that damage relationships.

Deception Does Not Equal Protection

Do you ever lie? Was your answer no? Is it possible *that* is a lie? ☺ Even if being honest is one of your values and even if you are not aware of it, you have lied. All human beings lie. On average, people lie once or twice a day (DePaulo and Kashy 1998; Kashy and DePaulo 1996). Why do we lie, even though it sometimes makes us feel guilty?

Not all lies are bad. Lies can sometimes be kind, and they can deescalate conflict. We typically lie about feelings, attitudes, and opinions. We lie to ourselves as well as to others, although lying to ourselves is not as easy as it sounds, because we almost always figure it out!

We lie to avoid punishment or blame or to gain advantage over others. We lie to get out of difficult situations. We lie to protect our maladaptive coping strategies (like using substances, spending money, an eating disorder). We often lie to ourselves in hopes of easing a painful truth. And yet deception is not protection. We often think lying helps us, but actually it likely pushes others away, and the disconnection that results hurts us. Think about some of the lies you have told over the past week or so and answer the questions in the following exercise.

Table 10.1: Lies, Consequences, and New Behaviors

Describe the lie	Positive consequences	Negative consequences	Consistent with values (yes or no)	Alternative behavior

What have you discovered about your lies? Is there something to learn?

Indirect Communication

"Indirect communication" is saying something in a way that hides our true intentions and allows us to avoid responsibility for what we are saying (Lynch 2018b). Indirect communication usually makes things worse, leads to hurt feelings, ☺ and can lead to distrust. Imagine you have plans with a friend. When the day comes, you don't want to go, but you don't want to hurt their feelings by saying that, so you hide your true intention (cancelling) by suggesting, "Hey, you must be exhausted after the day you described. How about we go another day, when you aren't so tired?" You have plausible deniability if your friend says, "Don't you want to go?" You would just reply, "Of course I want to go! I was just trying to be considerate of you." What do you think the chances are that your friend believes you? A. 0%. B. 1%. C. 1.5%

Have you ever had trouble asking for help even if it is something that's not a big deal? Perhaps you figured you could do it yourself—or *should* do it yourself. Perhaps you felt that hearing no would be more painful than not asking, even if that leads to you feeling alone and unsupported. Perhaps you indirectly let someone know you needed help but you did not ask: "I hope I can move these boxes in the house and still have time to go to the movies."

Have you ever not wanted to do something but didn't want to upset someone, so you did not respond directly? Have you ever struggled to be direct with someone because you worry that your honest feedback will upset them and make them not like you? Perhaps you've gotten upset because someone didn't do something when you thought they should have understood what you wanted them to do? You clearly said, "The dishes need to be washed before I can cook dinner." Thirty minutes later, when the dishes are still not washed, you angrily say, "I guess no one wants me to cook dinner!"

Avoiding direct communication might feel easier, but it can be harder for others to deal with. It can damage relationships and block genuine connections.

Disguised Demands

Disguised demands are a form of indirect communication. You want something (maybe you want your friend to stop giving you feedback), and you demand this, but in an indirect way that gives you plausible deniability. In other words, there is a secret desire to control (you want your friend to obey you). Sometimes this desire is so secret that it is even kept a little secret from yourself. ☺ But remember, it is very hard to lie to yourself or keep a secret from yourself! There are two forms of indirect communication that function to stop feedback and they signal disengagement indirectly. Disguised demands ask something of the person you are communicating with, without actually asking them. They might not even know you are asking something of them. There are two common forms of disguised demands that can be helpful to recognize. They are called "pushbacks" and "don't hurt me's" (Lynch 2018, 330).

Table 10.2: Disguised Demands
(Lynch 2018b)

	Pushback	Don't Hurt Me
Hidden Message	1. I'm not telling you what to do. 2. *But* you better do what I want! (You better do what I say or I will make life difficult for you!)	1. You don't understand me. 2. You are hurting me. (If you cared about me, you would stop pressuring me!)
Tone of Voice	Aloof, sarcastic, matter-of-fact, contemptuous, cold.	Wounded, whining, begging, sighing, using a very soft voice, overly friendly, sickly sweet.
Facial Expression or Body Posture	Flat or stony face, silent treatment, scowling, hostile stare, walk away, eye roll, disgust, cold, sharp, sarcastic, sneer, mock, snicker.	Hiding face with hands, hair, hat. Pouting, sulking, frowning, head down, eyes down, brooding, crying. Cringing, furrowing brow, having a pained expression on one's face.
Reaction from Others	Threat response (i.e., they want to run away or avoid, or fight and start pushback war). The feedback stops.	Caregiving response or treating you fragilely (i.e., others try and make you feel better by apologizing, validating, or soothing in some way). They stop giving you the feedback.
Function	*Both* attempt to control the behavior of others or block feedback. The disguised demand is to stop others from asking you to do something differently or to stop others from telling you something you don't want to hear *without* you saying it directly (i.e., you get to deny it if you want to!). The function of pushback and don't hurt me is to avoid taking responsibility and may be a way to put the blame on others.	
Downsides!	Other people avoid you because of fear of revenge or end up walking on eggshells around you. You lose out on helpful feedback.	Other people can see you as fragile or incompetent and end up walking on eggshells around you. You lose out on helpful feedback.

Got it? Now let's have some more fun! Read the story below and decide if Suzi communicates directly or with a pushback or with a don't hurt me. 😊

Suzi's boyfriend, Willis, was visiting from out of state. One night they watched a TV chef make a delicious-looking chicken dinner. Willis said, "We should have this one night this week. I'll be happy to make it." Suzie had a rule: she never ate any food that she didn't watch being made. She didn't want to tell him that, so in a very quiet voice, Suzi said, "But you know I'm at school late every day." Willis responded, "Don't worry! I'll make it by myself. I know how hard you work and how important that is to you. It's one way I can show you how much I love you." She knew he was being really sweet, but Suzi responded with a soft whine, "I don't want you to have to do it all by yourself. If you really cared about me, you'd know I'm too stressed to think about all this now. It's just too much." She curled up into a ball and put her face in her hands. At a loss, Willis rubbed her shoulder. "Hey, why don't we make it on Saturday, when you can be here. It'll be a nice thing to do together." Suzi realized that once he backed off, she felt instant relief, but she also saw that Willis looked a bit dejected.

What signal was Suzi giving to Willis?

_____

Suzi first needed to recognize that her don't-hurt-me response was a disguised demand. She wanted to control what she ate and what ingredients were in it and who was cooking that dinner. She was attempting to control her boyfriend too. Suzi realized that by insisting on control over all meals, she was going against her core value of connection and a growing value of flexibility. Suzi recognized that controlling this meal by telling Willis that he did not understand her feelings and he did not care about how stressed she would be if he insisted on cooking dinner for her, worked against these values.

From all that she had read, Suzi knew that she needed to be open and honest with her boyfriend about her desires for control. She explained to Willis that she felt the need to control the food because her eating disorder made her fear that she could not trust other people when it comes to food preparation. She told him that she does trust him and she would not want to communicate otherwise. She added that she knows he was only trying to be caring when he offered to cook for her and that she appreciates his willingness to put forth that kind of effort.

Finally, Suzi did some self-enquiry as she recognized how she had energy when she thought about Willis's cooking dinner for her while she was at school. She had a lot of energy when she thought about not being able to monitor the cooking process. She asked herself "what makes it difficult for me to accept the love and support from others? What makes it difficult for me to show that I trust loved ones?" And she felt more energy, something she felt the desire to run from, which she learned was a sign that there was some learning and growing for her to do here. Woohoo!! ☺

Now it's your turn! Think about a recent time when you had secret desires for control that took you away from your values, and use the following worksheet to try out this skill:

Worksheet 10.2: Skills for Disguised Demands

Describe the underlying circumstance:

_____

_____

Be aware of your secret desire for control. What were you trying to control?

_____

_____

What was your social signaling?

_____

_____

What are your values that you want to guide your actions?

_____

_____

How might you increase connection by being open and honest about your desires for control? How can you say what you really mean?

_____

_____

_____

Practice self-enquiry to learn and grow:

_____

_____

_____

Now let's take a look at pushbacks. Let's see if you can apply the above skills with Amy's use of a pushback in her desire to control. This is not a test—it's just practice.

Last summer, when Amy was attending an out-of-state science program for a month, her older sister, Rachel, came to visit for a long weekend. Amy often felt responsible for Rachel's happiness, and she wanted everything to be perfect for the visit. She made careful plans for the weekend, but she didn't plan where they would go to dinner Friday night. She wanted to appear flexible, as her sister often teased her (gave her feedback) about how much she planned. On Friday morning, Rachel asked if she could help with anything, and Amy suggested that she make reservations for dinner that night. As Rachel happily Googled "restaurants near me," Amy noticed that she felt irritated. She didn't want to eat inside or at a restaurant that didn't serve organic food or one that was too expensive. And she didn't want sandwiches.

Amy asked Rachel, with condescension in her voice, "Of course, I know you'd only consider restaurants with organic choices and outdoor seating?"

What was Amy trying to control?

_____

_____

What was Amy social signaling?

_____

_____

The more Amy asked questions, the less enthusiastic Rachel was. She asked, "Amy, would you prefer to do this yourself?" Amy said, "You're the one who offered to help." Rachel's face fell, and Amy realized that even though she wanted her sister to help, her inner desire for control was getting in the way of connecting with Rachel.

Which of Amy's values could guide her actions in this situation?

_____

_____

How might Amy increase connection by being open and honest about her desires for control?

_____

_____

What self-enquiry questions might help Amy learn and grow?

_____

_____

Communicating Based on Secret Desires for Control

Now that you have a better understanding of pushbacks and don't hurt me's and how they are a type of indirect communication called "disguised demands," let's look at other ways desire for control can show up. Think about the following questions as you work to identify your own desire for control (Lynch 2018b).

- Have you ever wanted someone to stop giving you feedback (positive or negative), or wanted someone to stop expressing how they feel toward you (angry, proud, and so on)?

- Have you ever wanted someone to help you—and you think that they should *know* you need help without your asking for it?

- How about times when you've wanted others to recognize how hard you've had it and therefore not pressure you to do anything or to change?

- Or maybe you've wanted others to appreciate your good intentions, sacrifices, and how hard you work?

- Have you wanted someone to validate you, soothe you, or even treat you as though you are fragile?

- Have you ever secretly wanted to punish someone or make them realize their shortcomings for not doing things the way you believe they should—or fast enough?

- Have you wanted vengeance for a perceived wrongdoing? (It can be particularly hard to admit this last one, even to ourselves.)

- Have you ever wanted to sabotage the efforts of others to win or to prove a point?

- Have you ever wanted to leave a social interaction or wanted others to leave so you could be left alone? (Many people can relate to that one.)

- Have you wanted people—or even the world—to change, to fit how you think things should be or so that you can get what you want? Perhaps you just want others to think or act as you do. You're correct about this, so why wouldn't they, right? 😊

- Have you ever wanted to change the topic just to avoid potential conflict?

These are common examples of secret desires for control. You likely won't relate to all of them, but which ones *do* you relate to? When you find yourself acting on thoughts like this, ask yourself if the behavior is in line with your values? Would you want others interacting with you like that? Would you encourage a child to act like that? If others knew your secret desires, would you be distressed? Perhaps there is something to learn about yourself here. Let's see how John notices his urges for control and how he used the RO DBT skill ROCKs ON.

John had a busy week ahead of him and could barely fit his training runs into his schedule. On top of that, his wife, Julia, was out of town Monday and Tuesday on business. He was stretched to his limit. On Tuesday night, soon after Julia returned home, their son, Ryan, told them that he needed a poster board and certain markers to complete an assignment for Thursday. Ryan apologized, saying he hadn't realized how quickly the assignment was approaching, and he was stressed about getting a good grade. John secretly wanted Julia to offer to take Ryan to the store, because clearly his schedule was already overwhelmed. However, Julia said, "John, could you take him to get it? I just barely got home, and I have so much to do for work tomorrow." His first thought was that it was ridiculous—She knows I have to run in the morning! But from his work in RO DBT, John realized this was a good time to work through the ROCKs ON skill.

Handout 10.1: Flexible Mind ROCKs ON
(Lynch 2018b)

R: *Resist* the urge to control other people.

O: Identify your interpersonal effectiveness goals and degree of *Openness*.

C: *Clarify* the interpersonal effectiveness goal that is your priority.

K: Practice *Kindness* first and foremost.

ON: Take into account the *Other* person's *Needs*.

This is how John worked through ROCKs ON by writing in his journal:

Yeah, I see that I want to control everything, but I have to Resist the urge to control Julia. I have to look at my interpersonal effectiveness goals, decide which is my priority here, and gauge my Openness to sticking to that goal. I really wish Julia would take Ryan to the store (objective effectiveness), and I'm hinting that she needs to, but why? She barely walked in the door, she's tired, and she has meetings at work to prepare for, and I'm so focused on my running—it is important.... But my value of connection is also important here. I want her to know that I'm a team player (relationship effectiveness). And I want to know that I'm a team player (self-respect effectiveness), and I want all three of them to know that they're more important to me than a five-mile training run. After all, what do I need to learn about really living my values? I mean, truly, what's more important: Julia and the kids or my race times (self-enquiry effectiveness)? What's next—right: Clarify. I'm working so hard on our marriage right now, so I think relationship effectiveness is most important here.

With ROCKs ON, I must put Kindness above desires for control. Kindness is humility in action. It's about showing I care, treating others as I want to be treated. Putting it that way really makes me want to put Julia first and to sacrifice for her, without expecting anything in return. We really are better together. I know how I felt when I saw her pull into the driveway today—I love her so much. I don't want to do anything to harm our relationship. What was I thinking when I secretly tried to get her to take Ryan to the store? No. No. Don't beat yourself up about this. I reacted automatically, but self-enquiry worked. I'm okay.

Okay, last step: the Other person's Needs. Julia needs to get to bed early. She never sleeps well in hotels. She always does so much for all of us—if anyone needs anything, she's there. So if she flat-out asked me to take Ryan, she must be exhausted. No more doubts about this. I'll take him.

The next morning, John took Ryan to the store before school. As they left the house, he could see in Julia's eyes how much she appreciated it. And he had a great time talking with Ryan about the project. He hadn't realized his son's passion for his topic, and Ryan seemed especially happy to discuss it with him. And John realized how happy he was spending that time with Ryan.

Ready to give ROCKs ON a try? Think about a time when you indirectly socially signaled due to your secret desire for control, and think about how you could instead enhance kindness and social connection.

Worksheet 10.3: ROCKs ON

Resist the urge to control people by first recognizing it:

_____

_____

Identify your interpersonal effectiveness goals and degree of *Openness*:

Relationship effectiveness: How do you want the other person to feel about you after the interaction?

_____

_____

Self-respect effectiveness: How do you want to feel about yourself after the interaction?

_____

_____

Objective effectiveness: What results or changes do you want to occur after the interaction?

_____

_____

Self-enquiry effectiveness: What do you imagine the other person's primary objective is, and what do you imagine their needs and desires will be during the interaction?

_____

_____

Clarify the interpersonal effectiveness goal that is your priority:

_____

_____

Practice *Kindness* first and foremost. What can you do to be kind instead of control?

_____

_____

Take into account the *Other* person's *Needs*. What are their needs and wants?

_____

_____

Way to go! Remember just being aware of your indirect social signaling is the first step. You can decide what you want to do about it from there. ☺ You might even need to ask others for feedback about your signaling in order to learn and grow.

Are You with Us?

Boy, are you learning a lot about social connection! Woohoo! Social flexibility, social connection, and now social engagement. Are you sensing a pattern here? As you know, us humans—we need each other. Our social connections are important to our survival. We need them even if we think we don't want them. You're learning the ways we all socially signal that can push others away, often through indirect communication, even when it's not our intention. Next you'll learn more about communication and finally enhancing intimacy. ☺ Have fun!

CHAPTER 11

Building Close Personal Bonds Through Communication and Feedback

Now that you're practicing what you've learned about social signaling, you'll learn key skills for building and deepening relationships. We'll also explain how the need for intimacy differs from person to person and how this impacts a relationship. We'll describe how you can develop reciprocal communication with others that can increase mutual closeness and bring about more intimacy in your relationships. And—oh, yeah—we'll describe how to stay open and allow feedback from others. Listening to and learning from feedback will help you to improve or maintain relationships that are important to you.

Building Relationships with Match+1, (Lynch 2018b)

In order to get to know somebody, or get closer, you have to reveal personal information. This signals to others that you trust them and have good intentions, especially if your facial expression matches your words (see also the DEEP skill in chapter 6).

Let's see how Amy's responses in conversations with three different people influenced what happened at the end.

Scenario 1

Amy enters a café; a waiter approaches.

W: How is your day going?

Amy: Fine.

W: Have you done something interesting today?

Amy: Nothing special.

The waiter takes the order and leaves.

Scenario 2

Amy encounters a coworker, Maria, at lunch. She isn't sure if she wants to become friends with her.

Maria: How is your day?

Amy: Fine. What about you?

Maria: Rough morning. I was up too late last night, so it was hard to get up and come to work.

Amy: What about this afternoon?

Maria: Tired. I wish I could just go home.

Amy: How late do you have to stay today?

Maria: We'll see. [She checks her watch.] Have to go now. Have a good day. [She walks away.]

Scenario 3

Amy gets home from work. Her sister is already there.

Rachel: How was your day?

Amy: Tedious as usual. But a new guy started today. Seems nice. How was yours?

Rachel: Traffic was awful, so I was late. Everyone stared at me when I walked in. I felt awful.

Amy: Know what you mean. It happened to me the other day. Someone even commented: "Late again." I wanted to crawl under a rock.

Rachel hugged Amy.

You can see how in scenarios 1 and 2, the conversation did not build a reciprocal relationship or increase the closeness between Amy and the other person. In scenario 2, she asked lots of questions but didn't disclose any personal information, which shut down their conversation. By contrast, the conversation in scenario 3 brought Amy and Rachel closer. They matched the other's level of self-disclosure and shared increasingly personal experiences at each stage. That's what Match+1 is (Lynch 2018b).

Match+1 is a skill you can use to get to know someone or deepen a relationship. You have to share something personal about yourself for others to respond to you in a more personal way. If you reveal feelings, thoughts, memories, and experiences, it signals to others that you are a trustworthy person.

Just asking the other person questions, as Amy did in scenario 2, does not deepen relationships. They might be put off and find the questions intrusive. And a person who asks questions but doesn't reveal anything can appear arrogant, controlling, and secretive.

How much you reveal in Match+1 will depend on how well you already know the person and how much you want to deepen the relationship. When first getting to know somebody, it's better to hold off on the really personal stuff. Start with general topics. The English are famous for starting every conversation by talking about the weather. If you are not English, chose a general topic that you don't feel emotional about. Anything spring to mind?

Getting to know someone well takes time, and people vary in how comfortable they are with self-disclosure. You yourself might find it uncomfortable. But that is why Match+1 is so helpful. It guides you through the process, teaching you how, when, and in which sequence you should reveal your personal information. Use handout 11.1: Match+1 to walk through each step and build your relationships.

Handout 11.1: Match+1

1. If you are feeling anxious before meeting someone, *activate your social-safety system.*

2. Greet the other person.

3. Reveal something about yourself to another person. Chitchats are essential when you first meet others. Start with something general, like something about your day or week.

4. Listen to how the person responds and then "match" their level of self-disclosure or go one level higher (see the table below, the Intimacy Level Continuum, for more on this).

5. Share less-personal details with people you don't know well. Talk about sports, politics, weather, work, school.

6. Remember that Match+1 mostly focuses on revealing personal information about yourself, and less about asking personal question about the other person—especially if you don't feel ready to be asked similar questions yourself.

7. With people you already know well, share thoughts and feelings. The closer you feel with them, the more you can share some emotionally charged events, judgments, and personal opinions.

8. Use *I* statements if you are revealing your feelings, thoughts, and beliefs so that another person knows that you are taking responsibility for them.

9. As intimacy with the other person develops, you can start sharing embarrassing events and vulnerable emotions. Revealing your deepest vulnerable emotion that you have not previously expressed, while making a commitment to the relationship that might include some serious self-sacrifice, will mean that you're at your highest (maximum) possible and desired level of intimacy. Use the table below, the Intimacy Level Continuum, to orient yourself to which level of intimacy you have with the other person. If you want to get to know them better, increase the personal information you share by going one level up (+1 in the table) over the level they shared.

Match+1 Intimacy Level Continuum

Intimacy Level	Match or +1	What to Do and Say
Low	Match	Talk about general topics without expressing personal emotions: weather, traffic, fashion, restaurant reviews.
	+1	Reveal personal values, opinions, and goals about general topics: climate change, politics, human rights, or talking about socially desirable preferences.
Medium	Match	Reveal true personal feelings and judgments, some of which might not be socially desirable, like "I hate people who aren't punctual."
	+1	Openly express feelings and judgments about personal relationships, even when emotions are running high (crying; expressing distress, anxiety, and anger)
High	Match	Openly express affection and desire for closeness to the other person. Share shameful and embarrassing personal events. Show vulnerability.
	+1	Openly express intense affection and commitment for a long-term relationship. Express most vulnerable emotions that have not been expressed before. Show readiness to make sacrifice for the other person.

10. Remember that the level of disclosure is influenced by your or the other person's mood, how rested or busy you are, the state of physical health, topic of conversation, where you are meeting (in public or private), and each person's experiences in past relationships.

11. Persevere. Match+1 is based on multiple interactions. Don't stop giving personal details just because the other person doesn't respond immediately.

12. Practice Match+1 whenever you can and whenever you want to get close (or closer) to someone. It takes a few meetings with the same person for communication to become more intimate. Don't rush it, but also don't get stilted in how you express yourself.

13. Remember, closeness takes time.

Building Relationships by Adjusting to Different Needs for Intimacy

People vary in their needs for intimacy. What's just right for one may be too cold or too hot for others. (Hmm, isn't there a children's story about that? Someone named Goldilocks? But we're off track. Back to the topic.) Some people want a lot of closeness, and others prefer less. There is no right or wrong amount. What feels warm and fulfilling to you may feel smothering to someone else.

Imagine that you're practicing Match+1, and the other person doesn't respond when you try to increase intimacy past a certain level. You want to be closer than they do. There could be many reasons for this, but one is that they have a lower maximum level of desired intimacy than you do. When someone you see as a close connection turns down an invitation, doesn't call as frequently as you would like, or participates in activities without you, you may feel rejected or think they don't care. But it could be that your intimacy needs are just different.

An important step in improving relationships is to understand, appreciate, and validate the other person's style of intimacy. Let's look at some examples.

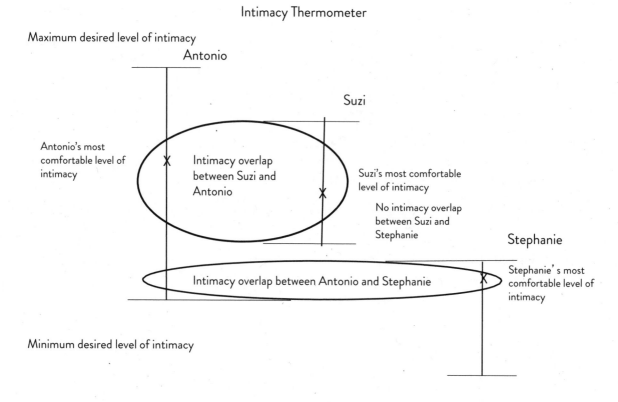

Figure 11.1

Antonio, Suzi, and Stephanie all know each other, and Antonio and Suzi have gotten to be friends. In the intimacy thermometer (Lynch 2018b, 425, fig 10.1), notice that Antonio's *maximum* desired level of intimacy is greater than Suzi's (at times he wants to be far more close than she can stand), and her *minimum* desired level of intimacy is higher than Antonio's (at times he is happy with a level of interaction that feels cold to her). Think how confusing that could be for Suzi! If Antonio is at his highest level of comfortable intimacy, Suzi feels smothered, and if he backs off to his lowest level, she feels deprived! Maybe you've been in that situation before. The good news is that there's a wide range of overlap. When you are building a relationship, part of what you're figuring out is the range of intimacy where you're both comfortable, so both of you can have your needs met. It's rare that your ranges will exactly match. But when there's an overlap, you can make it work. On other hand, there's only a small bit of overlap between Antonio's lowest level and Stephanie's highest. They might strike a note occasionally, when they're comfortable with each other.

Sometimes there is no overlap. In figure 11.1, Stephanie's maximum desired intimacy is below Suzi's minimum. Suzi often finds Stephanie distant, and Stephanie thinks Suzi is too needy.

Antonio enjoys talking with Suzi about his sister, and he likes how she shares stories that show how close she is to her family. Unfortunately, Suzi rarely hangs out with him, saying she is busy with school. He struggles with feeling rejected by Suzi, though when she does meet him for coffee or lunch, he's excited.

As for Stephanie, Antonio is close to giving up on the relationship. When she's around, she's fun and interesting, although she doesn't share much about herself, and she rarely calls or texts. Stephanie realizes he's frustrated with her, but what can she do? There are times when she finds him too talkative and prying, but sometimes she enjoys his company.

Connections are easier when there is a lot of overlap in desired intimacy levels. But it's not necessary, if you're both aware of the differences and willing to work with them. If you desire less intimacy than the other person, you'll need to work harder at times—for example, by increasing the ways you express affection; finding more time to spend with them; perhaps increasing touch (holding hands or other contact); sharing more of your thoughts, feelings, and experiences; and finding more activities you both enjoy. If you desire more intimacy than they do, you'll likely need to understand that you won't reach your maximum level of intimacy. You can do this by accepting (without resentment) that they have different preferences for intimacy, focusing on enjoying the times you share, and finding other ways to meet your intimacy needs (such as by spending time with other friends, with family, or with a pet).

What about you? Think about your relationships. Do you feel smothered in some? Ignored? Could this be due to different levels of intimacy? Consider these questions:

- Do you wish a friend or acquaintance called or texted you more often? Or do you think that they don't care enough, because you don't hear from them as much as you'd like?

- When a friend reaches out to you, do you think that they take up too much of your time? Or are you surprised they contacted you at all, because you thought they were pulling away or not interested in a friendship?

- Does a friend stay at about the same Match+1 level without reciprocating when you try to increase the level of intimacy? Or do they move up the Match+1 levels faster than you are ready for?

In worksheet 11.1, Working with Different Needs for Intimacy, list the relationships that you experience as too "hot" and smothering and those you experience as distant or less caring than you'd like? Consider this—do you enjoy this person and like spending time with them despite the stress of not having the same needs for intimacy? If so, the relationship is probably worth saving. Use the handout to work through different ways you can try to match more closely the other person's desired levels of intimacy and maintain the relationship.

Worksheet 11.1 Working with Different Needs for Intimacy

Describe relationships in which the other person wants to be closer to you than you want to be with them. (Too much intimacy; you might feel smothered.)

_____

_____

How can you be more open to closeness in these relationships? (Perhaps share more about your thoughts and feelings, increase touch, tell them about your own desires and be open to accepting their different desires, and find ways to spend more time together and ways to ask for time apart when you need it.)

_____

_____

_____

_____

Relationships in which the other person feels distant. (You feel rejected.)

_____

_____

How can you cope with less intimacy than you want to maintain these relationships? (Can you meet some of your intimacy needs with family, other friends, or pets; change your expectations of what a relationship means with this friend; accept the differences between you without harsh judgments of either of you; or prioritize moments that are important to share?)

_____

_____

_____

_____

So how many friendships do you need in life? It's quality not quantity that matters. Just having one close friend you trust, feel safe with, and can depend on when things get tough can fulfill your life. Isn't that what the friends are for? (I think I hear music playing—isn't there a song about that?) And you can develop friendships at any time, at any age, and under any circumstance. But if you want to build relationships or improve them, you need a few important skills. Let's start with two: (A) be open to the possibility that there will be times when you're wrong about your opinions, and (B) stay open to feedback, even when it hurts.

Chill Break!   Hey, time for a break! The idea of this book is to learn and practice as you go. So now might be a really good time to check in with your friends or family—or go to a social event, play, and meet new people. You can practice Match+1!

How to Improve Yourself and Your Relationships by Accepting Feedback

If you want to improve friendships, allow and consider feedback from others. What they think matters! And we all have blind spots. In a workplace, people who are open to critical feedback are highly effective employees (Ashford and Tsui 1991; Smither et al. 2005). They learn about themselves, alter their behavior (when needed), improve relationships, and adapt to an ever-changing world. Next time you receive feedback, listen and decide if you can learn from it. Remember, we need both criticism and praise to develop ourselves.

Yes, feedback can be a bummer (hard, yuck) when it feels like someone is criticizing you. It can be verbal, nonverbal (an eye-roll, a frown, a dismissive hand movement), or situational (a driver honks the horn at you for jaywalking). Let's see John's example.

When John refused to go to the barbecue, his wife, Julia, said, "This is the third time you're turning them down. They'll stop inviting us. We'll lose our friends because they'll think you are avoiding them." John was furious: "You don't understand. I can't do it." He walked outside in protest, his whole body tense. He noticed his heart racing and tight breathing, and did self-enquiry for a few minutes. He asked himself:

- *Am I feeling angry, numb, or emotionally shut down?*

- *Did I walk away in response to Julia's feedback?*

- *Did I respond immediately, without thinking it through?*

- *Do I feel a strong desire to explain myself?*

- *Am I automatically blaming Julia for my reactions?*

- *Am I closed to hearing her feedback?*

- *Is there something that I can learn from her feedback?*

How to Stay OPEN to Feedback

A physical reaction (body tension, a pounding heart) to feedback signals that you might be in a closed mind-set, unable to fully hear what someone is telling you. This is the time to practice being radically open to that feedback—be willing to be wrong, without losing your perspective or automatically giving in. You need to let go of mistrusting people who are giving you feedback. How many times have you thought negatively about someone only to realize later that you were wrong, that you'd misjudged them. Remember: "Just because I think it doesn't mean that it's true." Holding grudges or not letting go of past hurts can keep you closed to fully listening to feedback. Let go of all that to give yourself a chance to learn and improve your relationships (see also chapter 8). Use the steps in the handout 11.2 to stay open to feedback (adapted from Lynch 2018b).

Handout 11.2: Stay Open to Feedback

1. Acknowledge that you are receiving feedback (verbal or nonverbal).

2. Notice if you're feeling tense and defensive. Label emotions (anger, annoyance, sadness, fear) and action urges (an urge to walk away, retaliate, deny, or shut down).

3. Check if you're in Fixed or Fatalistic mind (see chapter 7). Is your response "yeah, but …"; "what's the point?"; "they aren't trying to help me"; or "anything I say is futile, as I will be shut down"?

4. Use self-enquiry to compassionately question your automatic responses. It can help block avoidance or keep you from blaming others, the situation, or the world.

    - Am I jumping to respond to feedback or questions without considering it?

    - Am I holding my breath or breathing more quickly? Has my heart rate changed?

    - Do I feel a strong desire to explain myself?

    - Am I feeling numb or emotionally shut down?

    - Am I automatically blaming something or someone else for my reactions?

5. Change body posture to facilitate openness—slow deep breathing, closed-mouth smile, use eyebrow wags, lean back rather than forward (practice Big 3+1).

6. Practice *fully* listening. Let go of denial, past hurts, and assumptions about what they're saying. Don't insist they listen to you before you listen to them. Don't rehearse your responses or give up if it does not go as you planned. Give yourself and the other person time. Take a break if the situation is getting emotionally charged.

7. Encourage openness by silently repeating:

    - *There may be something to learn from this feedback.*

    - *There may be some truth in what is being said.*

    - *Being open does not mean approval or that I must abandon my prior beliefs.*

Stay engaged. Surf the urges to abandon the relationship, walk away, or avoid. Go opposite: remain in the situation and thank the person for an opportunity to learn. Being open to corrective feedback is how we learn. Remember that a conflict can also bring you closer to the other person, and not everything has to be resolved at once.

After practicing self-enquiry, John went back inside. He thanked Julia for making him reflect on how his avoidance was impacting their relationships with friends. Together, they talked through how he could find a way to accompany her to the barbeque.

How to Learn from Feedback

When you have mastered staying open and listening to feedback, the next skill is to learn from feedback. This involves making sure you clearly understand what behavior the other person is suggesting you change, deciding whether to accept their suggestions, and then learning to alter your behavior. You can choose not to accept feedback (for example, if it doesn't fit your valued goals), though you should always consider it. Remember, learning from feedback and altering your behavior will help you improve or maintain relationships that are important to you. The feedback is well-meaning and from people who care about you, and it can help you avoid problems. Use the steps in the handout 11.3 to decide if you will adopt feedback and learn from it (adapted from Lynch 2018b).

Handout 11.3: Learning from Feedback

1. Clarify what the person would like you to change or do differently. Use an easy manner and ask for examples.

2. Repeat what you heard to confirm that your understanding is accurate. Be open to the possibility that you didn't get it right at first. Ask the other person to help you understand.

3. Once the feedback is clear, use the following questions to decide if you will accept it:

    *   Does the person have more experience in this area?

    *   Will accepting the advice help maintain my relationship with them?

    *   Will accepting it help me maintain other important relationships?

    *   Am I discounting the feedback to purposefully displease or punish the person?

    *   Will accepting it help me avoid significant problems (e.g., financial loss, employment difficulties, problems with the law)?

    *   Is the feedback something that I have heard from others before?

    *   Am I capable of making the suggested changes?

    If you mostly answered yes, go to the next step. If not, you can decide to decline the feedback.

4. Try out the new behavior. Use flexible mind VARIEs to boost your effectiveness (see chapter 6). Practice it again and again.

5. Self-soothe and reward yourself for being open and trying something new. Remember, the goal is to be open, not to be perfect.

And this is exactly what John did.

John thought, Julia's right that declining another invitation will jeopardize our friendship with them. And she didn't say it, but it would hurt our marriage as well. And she knows what she's talking about. She's the one who's good with people, not me. She just shines at a party. If I don't go, she'll feel down. And others have told me that I should socialize more. Okay. I'll go with her. And who am I kidding—there's bound to be a wide variety of food. I'll be fine. *He felt proud of himself for the decision, and when he told Julia, she gave him a kiss.*

Practice Opportunity

Use handout 11.1 to build your relationships using Match+1 and handout 11.2 to work out the differences in desired intimacy levels between yourself and the others. Track any feedback you received from others (start with today) using handout 11.4. Keep a record if you were open to feedback, if you accepted it, and what you have learned from it.

So Now You Know ...

Reciprocal communication helps you to get to know others or develop existing friendships. Knowing the other person's level of desired intimacy will help you maintain and improve relationships. And it's important to stay open to feedback from well-meaning people, even when it feels critical. We all need feedback to help us learn and become better people.

CHAPTER 12

Enhancing Intimacy

Your relationships will naturally have different levels of intimacy, and you might want to get closer to some people. In this chapter we'll look at ways to increase intimacy and maintain relationships. This means (yikes!) dropping your defenses, trusting, and taking the risk of being hurt. There are many ways to do this. Specifically, we'll consider characteristic behaviors in genuine friendships and how to cope with rejection, teasing, and validation.

Increasing Intimacy

Think of people who have a relationship that you admire, whether it's a really close friendship or a romantic relationship.

How do they interact that shows how they care for each other? Do they smile warmly at each other, make plans together, laugh together?

_____

_____

_____

What can you learn from them? How do you signal caring in your own relationships? How can you increase that?

_____

_____

_____

People can have close relationships in many different ways—there's no one right way. Observing relationships you admire is important, and can show you what's important to you in a close relationship. To help you develop that relationship, here are some key points.

Activate Social Safety

Remember in chapter 5 when you learned about cues and the emotional response systems associated with the cues? When you have an OC personality style, just *being* with people can be a cue that activates your threat system. Then, when in threat, you're focused on the "danger" in the situation—watching for signs of rejection or hostility—and you likely wouldn't notice if someone behaved in a friendly manner. What to do? The first step is to activate your social-safety system, using skills like Big 3+1 (see chapter 5).

Another way of activating your social-safety system is the loving-kindness meditation (LKM), which improves your mood and activates your social-safety system. Using LKM before social interactions can increase positive responses and feelings of social connectedness. While only a short six-minute exercise is needed, research shows that the more you practice, the stronger the effects. Remember it's about activating your social-safety system, nothing else (like how you feel toward someone else).

The following LKM script was designed specifically for OC individuals and is to be read aloud or listened to from a recording (Lynch 2018b, 108). Consider recording it on your phone so you can just listen whenever you need it.

Handout 12.1: Loving-Kindness Meditation

Getting seated. Find a comfortable seated position in a chair, on the floor, or on the sofa. The most important thing is that you find a position in which you feel alert and the chances of you drifting off to sleep are minimal. For the practice of loving-kindness, you can keep your eyes open or closed—the choice is yours—with the understanding that our goal is to remain awake, as best we can.

Noticing the breath. Once you find that position, begin by simply taking a breath—with awareness. Not trying to change the breath or fix it in some way, just being fully present with the full duration of the in-breath and the full duration of the out-breath. You may notice it most strongly in the nose and the throat. Some people notice the breath in the chest or the belly. Wherever the breath is most alive for you, just allow yourself to rest your awareness there. If your mind wanders away from the breath, which it is prone to do, then, without judgment, just bring yourself back to the next natural inhalation or exhalation.

Finding your heart center. And now, very gently, allow your awareness to move from your breath to your heart center. Into that place, right there, in the middle of the chest. Not as much the physical heart but that place where we tend to feel warm emotions. If you would like to do so, sometimes people find it helpful to gently place their open hand over the location of their physical heart, as this can help facilitate the practice.

As best you can, find a memory or feeling sense of a time when you experienced a strong sense of loving-kindness, either from someone or toward someone. It might have been the first day you met your life partner, the day a child or grandchild was born, a particular afternoon with your favorite pet, or a time when you felt warm appreciation after helping or being helped by someone. The idea is not to find the perfect experience or image; nor should you be concerned if you find yourself thinking of many different events or experiences. The idea is—as best you can—to re-create the warm, tender, or positive feelings associated with prior experiences of loving-kindness, and to allow these feelings to grow in your heart center. For just a moment, allow these feelings to grow.

Sending loving-kindness to a person you care about. And now, in your mind's eye, gently bring into focus an image of someone you care about, a person you already have existing warm feelings for, may feel love toward, or may feel a sense of positive connection with. It doesn't have to be a perfect relationship or one without conflict—the idea is to find an image or feeling sense of someone you know whom you already have warm feelings for. As best you can, hold this image or a feeling sense of this person in your heart center. And now, from the feelings of loving-kindness in the center of your chest, extend warm wishes to this person you care about. Using these phrases, silently repeat to yourself the following meditation, inserting the name of the person you care about (and we recommend that you don't change the wording of this):

May _____ be at ease.

May _____ be content with their life.

May _____ be joyful.

May _____ feel safe and secure.

Again, extending warm wishes of loving-kindness to them:

May _____ be at ease.

May _____ be content with their life.

May _____ be joyful.

May _____ feel safe and secure.

And again, from the source of loving-kindness in your own heart, extending well wishes to them:

May _____ be at ease.

May _____ be content with their life.

May _____ experience joy.

May _____ feel safe and secure.

And now, gradually allow the image or feeling sense of this person you care for to gently dissolve from your mind's eye, resting your attention back in your heart center, back into those feelings of warm loving-kindness—as best you can.

Sending loving-kindness to a person we feel neutral about. Bring to mind an image of someone whom you don't really know, someone you've at least seen once but don't feel any connection with one way or another. It could be your dentist, a supermarket clerk you've seen, or someone else of that sort. And again, as best you can, from your own heart, extending warm wishes of loving-kindness toward this person you hardly know about, saying silently:

May _____ be at ease.

May _____ be content with their life.

May _____ be joyful.

May _____ feel safe and secure.

Again, extending warm wishes of loving-kindness to this person you hardly know at all:

May _____ be at ease.

May _____ be content with their life.

May _____ be joyful.

May _____ feel safe and secure.

And again, from the source of loving-kindness in your own heart, extending well wishes to this person you barely know:

May _____ be at ease.

May _____ be content with their life.

May _____ be joyful.

May _____ feel safe and secure.

Ending the meditation. And now, with warm, loving care, gently turn your attention back to the sensations of your breath and your heart center, allowing the image or feeling sense of this person you hardly know to be released—allowing yourself to rest here, in this moment, with your feelings of warmth and kindness. You can carry with you throughout the day these warm feelings of love and kindness that you were able to generate, knowing that you can always find your heart center when needed and making a kindhearted commitment to integrate this practice of loving-kindness into your life, as best you can. And when you are ready, open your eyes and bring your attention back into the room.

You'll get the most from LKM if you use it daily. Practice before social interactions. Make a digital recording of the script and listen to it before you leave your home every day. Use the following worksheet to record your experiences (and you can download extra copies at https://www.newharbinger.com/48930).

Worksheet 12.1: Loving-Kindness Meditation Practice

Day	Situation	What Did You Notice?
M		
T		
W		
Th		
F		
S		
S		

Social Signals of Friendliness

When you want to signal friendliness, you use eyebrow wags (see chapter 5), warm smiles, openhanded gestures, a musical tone of voice, and context-appropriate touch. You nod your head and take turns in conversation.

SMILES, AUTHENTIC FACIAL EXPRESSIONS, AND LAUGHTER

You can smile in a genuine way only when you feel safe. When you interact with others, do you smile easily? A smile is a primary way of signaling friendliness, and even three- and four-year-old children recognize a genuine smile (Song et al. 2016). Which of the photos below shows a genuine smile?

A   B

Photos by Miles, L. & Johnston, L (2007)

If you said *B*, you're right. A genuine smile (also called a *duchenne* smile) involves not just lifting the corners of the mouth but also crinkling the sides of the eyes. It's like the smile involves the eyes. When interacting socially, activate your social-safety system (so you can send friendly signals to others), and remember to smile.

Along with a genuine smile, it is important for the rest of your face to express openness and friendliness so others know and trust you. (Review chapter 6 if you need a refresher on avoiding inhibited and disingenuous emotional expressions.) If you tend to not show emotions on your face, practice in the mirror. It will get easier the more you practice.

Try an expression of anger first. Think of something that once made you angry and show anger on your face, watching the effect in the mirror. Do the same for fear, sadness, curiosity, interest, and love.

Notice how your face feels with each expression. Does your face communicate the emotion you intend to express?

Laughing together—at funny jokes or things that happen—also helps create a bond between people. As with smiles, it's important to laugh genuinely, which means being willing to be playful and silly. In fact, the degree to which couples laugh together is an indicator of their satisfaction with the relationship (Gray et al. 2015; Kurtz and Algoe 2015). You're also more likely to disclose more information about yourself after laughing together (Gray et al. 2015). Reminiscing about times when you laughed together has a positive impact on relationships, even more than just remembering general positive experiences (Bazzini et al. 2007). There's something unique about laughter in strengthening relationships.

CHITCHAT AND MEANINGFUL TALK

Engaging in chitchat is an important part of connecting with someone. It helps at the start of a relationship, since you don't begin a new friendship by talking about your innermost feelings. Even with loved ones, you won't always or even mostly talk about deep topics. But to make a relationship closer, you'll move beyond chitchat—joking around, catching up with what's going on in their lives, and having meaningful conversations involving self-disclosure (Hall 2018). Being interested in the ordinary details of their life signals caring—asking about their day and listening to their thoughts about current events. Sometimes with people you know well you may talk mainly about tasks that need to be completed, which, while necessary, is not particularly helpful in building intimacy. On the Match+1 scale, chitchat would be the lower levels of intimacy, such as 1 to 4, as was discussed in the last chapter.

TOUCH

Friendly gestures like smiles and head nods (or saying things like "so good to see you!") are more powerful when combined with a hug or a touch on the arm. Touch increases intimate emotions like love, sympathy, empathy, and compassion. In general, touching is for those you are closest to: family, romantic partners, old friends, and pets.

SHOWING UP

Part of building meaningful relationships is sharing life experiences—big ones like graduations and birthdays and little ones like a casual conversation (Fehr 2008; Hall 2018). You have to show up, and here *showing up* means really being present and participating.

Sometimes the biggest challenge for OC folks is spontaneous invitations. Someone says, "Let's go get coffee" or "Let's go dancing," and even though you have nothing else to do, you decline—maybe making up an excuse—because it wasn't in your plans or you want to research salsa dancing and practice before you go out. (Does that sound like it happened to one of us who are writing this book? It did!) Practice being open and vulnerable and go! Will you make lots of mistakes when you're trying something new, especially something like salsa dancing? Of course you will! (Indeed, the salsa instructor in question said at one point, with a dramatic smile, "It'll be a miracle if you get this step.") We all make mistakes—taking it lightly and revealing your common humanity will help build the friendship.

BEHAVIORS OF GENUINE FRIENDS

There are a number of ways that genuine friends behave toward each other that strengthen their relationship. Think about a relationship that's important to you, preferably one outside your family, and then use the list in worksheet 12.2 (which you can also download at https://www.newharbinger.com/48930), to track which friendship behaviors you already practice and which you want to increase (Lynch 2018b, 426).

Worksheet 12.2: Genuine Friends

Put a check in column A for what you are currently doing. Then review the list again and put a check in column B for any you want to start doing or do more of.

A	B	Friendship behaviors
		Feel safe when together
		Trust each other
		Are willing to make sacrifices for each other without expecting anything in return or feeling resentful
		Look out for each other
		Stand by each other when the going gets tough
		Don't try to change each other
		Trust each other to do the right thing
		Respect each other's individual differences
		Care more about their relationship than material gain, personal achievement, or personal needs
		Are kind to each other
		Apologize to each other when unkind and strive to repair any damage that may have been done
		Are open to feedback, even when it hurts
		Take responsibility for their own emotions rather than blaming them on each other
		Are polite and respectful toward each other, especially during times of crisis or stress
		Are respectful of each other when they share inner feelings (e.g., don't yell, shout, belittle, or speak sarcastically toward each other)
		Don't bully, threaten, lie, or manipulate each other to get what they want
		Don't expect each other to be perfect
		Give each other the benefit of the doubt
		Fight fair

A	B	Friendship behaviors
		Don't automatically assume each other to be in the wrong when in conflict
		Admit to each other their own possible contributions to a conflict or disagreement
		Don't hold grudges
		Work out resentments, conflicts, or misunderstandings when they arise rather than holding a grudge or hoping the problem disappears
		Work together to solve problems, without keeping track of who has worked harder
		Respect each other's opinions
		Share their successes and failures
		Give each other time to express their views and openly listen to each other
		Give each other the gift of truth with kindness and tell each other what they really think or feel
		See each other as equals
		Show genuine emotions in front of each other (maybe even cry)
		Can tease each other (*Sneaky preview—this is a really important friendship skill and there's more to come about this!*)

Great! Make note of the behaviors you want to increase in a journal or worksheet 12.3 (below, and you can download it at https://www.newharbinger.com/48930) so you can keep track of when you practice them, and start thinking about how you'll make that happen.

Worksheet 12.3: Friendship Behaviors to Increase

Day of Week	Behavior to Increase	How I Practiced This Behavior
Mon	Gift of Truth	I shared with my friend that I thought the feedback she got from another friend (that she sometimes might come across as being too critical) might be helpful to her.

Building Relationships by Teasing (Yes, Teasing!)

There are different types of teasing, and one of them is teasing someone with feedback. Feedback often feels like a criticism, but friends can make it less of a big deal by pointing out flaws in a caring and playful way (Lynch 2018b). When friends tease in this way, it's a sign of closeness and comfort. It can increase intimacy between friends. And research confirms that teasing is a useful way of providing feedback or correcting inappropriate behavior. ("Look at this! Somebody still hasn't picked their clothes up off the floor. I wonder who that could have been." "Of *course* I'll get you something to drink! After all, I am at least six feet closer to the kitchen than you are.") Learning how to tease and be teased is an important part of healthy social relationships.

When someone teases you playfully with feedback, it shows that they're paying attention to you and have a genuine interest in you. It can also signal acceptance of your quirks (we all have them), which can build the relationship ("Of course, no appointments before eleven—you need your beauty sleep, after all). They know you well, and they care about you.

A good tease momentarily introduces conflict but then quickly reestablishes social connectedness. It starts with what seems like a critical comment—delivered with an unsympathetic voice tone (perhaps expressionless or arrogant), an intimidating facial expression (like a blank stare), and a stern gesture or body posture (finger wagging or hands on hips)—but it's followed by signals of playfulness (like giggling, eyebrow wags, and smiling) that deliver the message "it's not so serious and I care about you!" That friendly playfulness is crucial for a tease to be taken lightly and for it to increase the bond between people. The teaser is signaling that they know your relationship is strong and that they care about you deeply enough to give you important information (Lynch 2018b).

Warning! There is, of course, a *mean* tease that most people have experienced at one time or another. Mean teasing is not friendly. Even if the teaser says, "I'm just joking," everyone knows they aren't. The intention of a mean tease is not friendly feedback, and it's not a sign of caring. It's often about putting someone down or an indirect expression of anger.

Receiving Teases

People who are okay about being teased have an easy manner—they don't take themselves too seriously and can laugh (with their friends) at their foibles, gaffes, and mishaps. It's like they are saying, "We are all human, and I know you care about me." When teasing is playful and reciprocal, it is socially bonding. In fact, teasing is an important component of flirting, and couples who tease each other tend to be happier together (Brauer and Proyer 2018).

Research also suggests that teasing is a way of testing trust in the relationship: "Do you know that I truly care about you?" So when you can't take a tease, it may signal that you aren't open to feedback or that you are unsure of the relationship.

The best way to learn teasing is to practice. Look for opportunities to tease your family and others you see on a regular basis. Remember to start with an apparently serious comment, quickly followed by some kind of playful signal.

Time to practice—how would you tease a friend in the following scenarios? Assume it's in a close and caring relationship.

1. Your roommate is playing music while you're trying to study.

    _____

    _____

2. A friend is extremely anxious because friends are coming for dinner and one of the plates is chipped.

    _____

    _____

3. A friend says, "It's not that I'm upset about it, but I'm upset about it."

    _____

    _____

Here are some examples of teases for these scenarios. Remember to signal that it's a tease!

1. "Thanks so much for helping me pass this test by being *sooo* quiet while I study."

2. "Oh yes, that chip's going to ruin the food, and everyone will just leave because it's so horrific."

3. "I just love it when you're so clear about how you feel."

Coping with Rejection (Yeah, There's That)

To build friendships, you risk being rejected. For any number of reasons, you'll probably be rejected multiple times in your attempts to make friends. Our guess is you hate rejection, sometimes to the point that you don't want to risk getting close to others, and you stay lonely. But you know what? Being rejected happens anyway. You can't avoid it. It's part of being human.

Read this: "You're going to be rejected." What just happened inside you? Our guess is that you didn't jump for joy. Research shows that when someone rejects you, it triggers the same areas of the brain that are activated when you are physically hurt (e.g., Kross et al. 2011). It *does* hurt.

How to cope with rejection? Here's some suggestions:

- Remember that rejection is a universal experience. You'll be rejected, and you'll reject others too. It's a part of life. Congratulate yourself on taking risks.

- Is there something to learn from the rejection? It might be obvious: "Don't gossip harshly about a friend." If your emotions are stronger than you think is warranted by the situation, maybe there's also something to learn through self-enquiry.

- Rejection often involves a loss. What did you lose? Allow yourself to grieve and forgive (see chapter 9).

- When you experience a loss (a job, a relationship), you tend to see only the positive aspects of what you lost. That's the rose-colored-glasses effect. Remember the negative or less desirable points too.

- Rejection isn't always the end, nor does it mean what you want is unobtainable. It's often a change in direction or a "next."

- Different emotions can come from rejection. If you experience shame or anger, go opposite (see chapter 8).

- Get perspective. How would you comfort a friend who'd been rejected? Be as kind to yourself as you would be to a friend.

- Being rejected doesn't mean you are a total reject. Rejection is really kind of okay, if you think about it. If you taste six salad dressings and choose one you prefer, does that mean the others are bad? Of course not. So maybe the other person didn't appreciate your interests or values. That's what finding a friend is all about. So that one person was different from you—how about that!

- If you seek out friendships, you'll occasionally experience pain, but you'll also experience pain if you don't. Which path gets you closer to psychological health and your valued goals?

Conflict

Conflict is a part of relationships. Constructive conflict can deepen and strengthen connections. You may find conflict so uncomfortable that you want to end the relationship, or perhaps you see it as rejection. RO DBT emphasizes that when we feel uncomfortable, there may be something for us to learn. When there is conflict, be curious about the other person's point of view. Do you understand their perspective? If you disagree with them, ask yourself if it's consistent with your values to not be friends with someone you disagree with. Are you open to different points of view? You might also consider self-enquiry questions—what is there for you to learn?

To talk with someone when there's a conflict, use the PROVEs skill (chapter 6). It gives you a chance to work through conflict and maintain the relationship—and even strengthen it.

> **Chill Time**   Take a break. Relax. Play a game. You've worked hard, and it's time to take a breather. Indulge yourself a bit.

Validation

Wait! Did you *really* take a break? It's important to chill out and relax a bit and not always push, push, push. If you didn't really take a break, would you do it now?

Okay, on to validation. One of the most important and effective relationship skills is validation—letting someone know that you understand and accept their thoughts, emotions, impulses, actions, desires, or experience (Fruzzetti and Worrall 2010). Validation is a way to signal caring and to increase the closeness in the relationship. You show that you accept them as they are and give them a safe place to share their inner experiences. Validation also shows that you're paying attention to their social signals. Validation does not mean you *agree*, only that you *understand*. That's part of connecting.

Validation is just as important in maintaining relationships as it is in building them. A 2017 study found that slightly more than half the time, people confided their worries to people with whom they weren't particularly close, even people they met by chance, rather than to those closest to them. Surprised? Sharing worries and concerns is part of being close, so what's going on? The study suggests people who don't know you well are likely to show more interest, ask relevant questions, and be less apt to interrupt (Small 2017). They're more likely to be attentive (be validating). So validation is a sort of relationship glue.

The tricky thing about validation is that no matter how validating you think you are, it's the other person who decides if you actually were. Despite your best intentions, if the other person didn't experience what you said as validating, it wasn't. But that's okay. Listen to the feedback and try again.

There are different ways to validate, including being attentive, reflecting back, empathic mind reading, validating based on history, normalizing, signaling trust, and reciprocity. Let's consider each of these (Linehan 1997; Lynch 2018b).

Level 1: Being Attentive

Being attentive signals to the other person that you value them and want to learn about them—you spend time with them, nod your head, smile, ask questions, and make eye contact (in most cultures). Truly listening to what someone is saying is being attentive. This means not planning what you're going to say next or thinking of other things, like how much you want to go home and be by yourself. People can usually sense when you're distracted by your thoughts and not really listening to them, though the signs may be subtle.

It may seem odd, but we are sometimes *less* attentive with people we know well. It's called the "closeness-communication bias." If you know someone fairly well, you tend to think you know what they're going to say, so you don't listen as carefully (Savitsky et al. 2011). For example, if your spouse or parent brings up your struggles in recovery, you may make assumptions about what they're going to say based on past conversations about it. You may shut them down. That response may make it less likely that they'll share their worries with you again. Remember, listening to someone doesn't mean you have to agree with them. To truly make connections and deepen relationships, you have to be really present and try to understand them.

Level 2: Reflecting Back

"Reflecting back" simply means repeating to the other person what you heard them saying and doing so with interest and humility. This isn't just parroting what they said. It's a way you show that you want to understand their thoughts, experiences, and feelings.

Voice tone and social signals are part of the meaning of what someone says. If someone says, "I am so angry with you," and they wink, smile, and shrug their shoulders in an appeasement gesture, then what you reflect back is not the words, but the meaning the person has communicated to you. You know they're not really angry, so you wouldn't reflect back that they are, even though their words said differently. Perhaps you'd reflect back, "You're teasing me about being angry." Reflecting back can be particularly important when the social signaling might not match the words said or you're not sure what the person is communicating to you. Sometimes you can be sure you got the meaning, but you really haven't.

Imagine you're talking with Amy, who is feeling rejected because she wasn't invited to Jill's party. An example of reflecting back would be, "You're saying you feel rejected because you weren't invited to her party, is that right?" This may seem obvious to you, but it gives you a chance to check your understanding. Amy might say, "Yeah. It hurts." Your reflecting back has helped her feel understood and connected to you. But what if your understanding isn't correct? Amy might say, "No, not really. I'm upset because I think Jill's best friend, Angela, is telling lies about me. I'm worried that's why I wasn't included." You can now reflect back again: "Oh, so you're really upset because you think Angela is lying about you and hurting your friendship with Jill?" When done with true interest, reflecting back can show the other person that you understand and care.

So how do you respond when someone reflects back to you? Sometimes people who have an OC personality style find it hard to believe that others might understand what they are saying or feeling. True, no one can know *everything* about someone else, and your emotions may not be exactly like anyone else's, but we all know what emotions basically feel like. We're all human. When someone reflects back what you have said, think about it before you answer. Is it basically right? If so, let them know.

On the other hand, you may also have a tendency not to correct someone when they misunderstood you. It's just as important to connection to let someone know when what they heard is not what you meant to communicate. You're giving the gift of truth so others can know you. It's all part of connecting.

Level 3: Empathic Mind Reading

In empathic mind reading, you try to guess how someone else might be feeling or thinking. You do so with the understanding that you are just *guessing*, because—well, duh, 'cause you are. You can't really know what they're experiencing. So it's important to word your empathic mind read to show that you know you're guessing. Begin by saying something like "I'm guessing that..." "If I were in your shoes..." or "It seems like you might be..."

Imagine you're having lunch with Suzi. You're worried about her relationship with her boyfriend, which you've shared with her before. She says, "My boyfriend just got this great new job! He'll have more responsibility, and he gets a big raise. I'm so happy for him! He'll also get to travel a lot more, which he's excited about." With an empathic mind read, you might respond, "If I were in your shoes right now, I think I might have mixed feelings. Are you a bit sad that he'll be away more often?"

You might be wrong, but by trying to put yourself in your friend's shoes, you're signaling that you want to know how your friend is really feeling. Expect to get it wrong occasionally, and when you do, own it and repair if necessary.

Understanding someone else does not mean agreement or approval. For example, imagine that Suzi said that she appreciated what you said, but that she wanted to support Willis in his new job. You might say, "I understand that—and a good job is important. At the same time, I care about you, and I'm aware that his travel might be hard for you." In other words you can accurately mind read your friend yet still stand firm about what you believe is important.

Level 4: Validating Based on History or Biology

Level 4 recognizes that anyone with a similar background (or biology) would behave in a similar manner. Imagine that you're walking with Amy, and you suggest a shortcut through an alley. Amy looks upset and says, "No, I can't do that. I'm not going that way."

Validating Amy, you might say, "Oh, of course! I remember that you were robbed in an alley last year. Come on, let's walk this way instead."

Level 5: Normalizing

Validating someone's behavior as normal signals that how they behaved or emotionally responded is no different from how others would have reacted in similar circumstances.

When Amy's favorite teacher retires, she shares with you that she's sad but thinks it's silly, because he was just a teacher. You might say, "Of course you're sad. Anyone would be sad if their favorite teacher left." It's a way of saying, "Hey, we're with you in this human experience."

Level 6: Signaling Trust

Level 6 validation signals genuine belief, trust, and confidence in the other person, sometimes showing greater confidence in them than they have in themselves: "I'm sure you can open an account on your own." "I know that you can figure out the directions." "I think you can make this decision for yourself."

Level 7: Reciprocity

It's often not *what* you say but *how* you say it. You've heard that a lot throughout this workbook. Part of connecting with others and showing that you understand and care about their experience is in matching their intensity, tone, facial expressions, and gestures. You match their emotions. Imagine that your friend has just won an award. Which scenario makes it clear that you're excited and proud? (A) Sitting quietly in your chair with a slight smile and saying, "I'm so excited and proud," or (B) Jumping up when they enter the room, giving them a high five, smiling broadly, and saying, "I'm so excited and proud!"

Imagine a friend telling you that they just lost their job or a scholarship. What type of nonverbal signals are needed in this situation to match your friend's expression?

_____

_____

Don't Validate the Invalid

Sometimes, though, validation may not fit the context. Perhaps your friend becomes angry and quits a job she really needs, and her reasons for quitting don't make sense. You wouldn't want to say that you understand her behavior and that anyone would do the same. You don't want to validate what's not valid. When our behavior is not in our best interest or is even destructive, and we don't recognize that, we need someone to kindly point out our error and give corrective feedback.

Stephanie returned home following inpatient treatment, instead of continuing in residential care, as was recommended. She didn't follow her eating plan and quickly lost weight. Her nutritionist, parents, and the friends she'd made in treatment all validated how difficult it can be to make changes and how hard it can be to transition to home from an inpatient setting. They validated feelings such as fear and anger. They also talked with her about her decision to not follow her plan, though she insisted she was fine. She was furious and repeatedly insisted that they didn't understand her and didn't believe in her. Her friends, treatment team, and parents all told her that they cared about her and that they saw her engaging in eating-disordered behaviors. They said that they were expressing what they saw and doing it out of caring.

Was Stephanie validated? Yes. Her feelings were validated as her feelings, and the difficulty of the situation was validated. But her friends and family didn't validate her choices or behavior—that would have been lying to her. They couldn't say, "Yes, of course it's okay to not follow your eating plan. We can see you've got this under control." Not only would that be dishonest, but it would also be uncaring. Sometimes difficult feedback gives important information from caring people. They could say, "We understand that you think this way, but we don't agree," which would validate her experience while still giving her crucial feedback. Feedback about inaccurate thinking and perceptions can be lifesaving. Think about how important it would be to tell a fellow cave dweller, "That's not a sheep. It's a tiger!"

So Now You Know

In this chapter you learned ways to create and strengthen intimate relationships, including genuine friendships, through activating social safety, communication skills, showing up, and validation. You also learned how to cope with rejection and the importance of invalidation. Becoming comfortable with what you learned in this chapter may take a lot of practice. We hope you'll use it as a reference as you create your friendships and loving relationships.

CHAPTER 13

Not Really a Chapter, Not Really an Ending

Celebrate! You've come a long way. You've learned the importance of relationships in recovering from an eating disorder. You've learned about your personality style and how you form relationships. You've considered your values and valued goals, and you know these will change as you accomplish your goals and as time passes. You've considered the information that uncomfortable sensations and emotions can give you about yourself by practicing self-enquiry. You've learned how you might be using armor to protect yourself, which can block relationships; how social signaling impacts connections; and how to social signal in ways that build relationships. And you've practiced what you've learned and are using it to build a life you want to share with others. Congrats to you!

At the same time, finishing this workbook doesn't mean you're done. Learning about yourself and continuing to grow psychologically is a lifelong process. The skills you've learned here are tools to use in your personal growth and connections with others for many years to come. Good wishes to you from us— Ellen, Mima, and Karyn (and Tom and Erica Lynch, too!)—as we all practice radical openness.

Learn everything you can, anytime you can, from anyone you can; there will always come a time when you will be grateful you did. —Sarah Caldwell

Acknowledgments

While the list of people we want to acknowledge for their contributions to this book is enormous, we regret that we cannot directly thank each one of you. However, it is imperative, first and foremost, to thank our clients who have been vulnerable, open and giving in sharing themselves with us. Thank you for allowing us to use your personal stories as tweaked examples, in the hopes of helping others learn and grow. Thank you to our teams at Eating Recovery Center, The Dialectical Behavioral Therapies Center, and the Maudsley Center for Child and Adolescent Eating Disorders particularly Sam Bottrill and Charlotte Watson. We would also like to thank Michael Astrachan for his illustration and our team at New Harbinger Publications. While this might sound silly, ☺ the three of us would all like to thank each other for making this a surprisingly enjoyable process as the birth of this book required passion, dedication and vulnerability on all our parts and we became so much closer because of it. Love you guys! Of course, thank you to Tom for having the brilliance, creativity and heart to create this amazing treatment that has already helped so many. Thank you to Erica, for your consultation, edits, and constant support. We are grateful to the whole RO senior clinician team. We are for sure, better together.

References

Ashford, S. J., and A. S. Tsui. 1991. "Self-Regulation for Managerial Effectiveness: The Role of Active Feedback Seeking." *The Academy of Management Journal* 34, no. 2: 251–80. doi:10.2307/256442.

Bazzini, D. G., E. R. Stack, P. D. Martincin, and C. P Davis. 2007. "The Effect of Reminiscing About Laughter on Relationship Satisfaction." *Motivation and Emotion* 31, no. 1: 25–34. doi.10.1007/s11031-006-9045-6.

Brauer, K., and René T. Proyer. 2018. "To Love and Laugh: Testing Actor-, Partner-, and Similarity Effects of Dispositions Towards Ridicule and Being Laughed At on Relationship Satisfaction." *Journal of Research in Personality* 76: 165–76. doi.org/10.1016/j.jrp.2018.08.008.

Cardi V., Di Matteo R., Corfield F., and Treasure J. 2013. "Social reward and rejection sensitivity in eating disorders: an investigation of attentional bias and early experiences." *World Journal of Biological Psychiatry* Dec; 14, no. 8: 622–33. doi: 10.3109/15622975.2012.665479. Epub 2012 Mar 16. PMID: 22424288.

Costafreda, S. G., M. J. Brammer, A. S. David, and C. H. Y. Fu. 2008. "Predictors of Amygdala Activation During the Processing of Emotional Stimuli: A Meta-Analysis of 385 PET and fMRI Studies." *Brain Research Reviews* 58, no. 1: 57–70. doi.org/10.1016/j.brainresrev.2007.10.012.

Davis, F. C., M. Neta, M. J. Kim, J. M. Moran, P. J. Whalen. 2016. "Interpreting Ambiguous Social Cues in Unpredictable Contexts." *Social Cognitive and Affective Neuroscience* 11, no. 5: 775–82. doi.org/10.1093/scan/nsw003.

DePaulo, B. M., and D. A. Kashy. 1998. "Everyday Lies in Close and Casual Relationships." *Journal of Personality and Social Psychology* 74, no. 1: 63–79. doi:10.1037/0022-3514.74.1.63.

Ebner, N. C., Riediger, M., & Lindenberger, U. (2010). FACES - A database of facial expressions in young, middle-aged, and older women and men: Development and validation. *Behavior Research Methods, 42*(1), 351–362. doi:10.3758/BRM.42.1.351

Fehr, B. 2008. "Friendship Formation." In *Handbook of Relationship Initiation,* ed. S. Sprecher, A. Wenzel, and J. Harvey, 29–55. New York: Psychology Press.

Fruzzetti, A. E., and J. M. Worrall. 2010. "Accurate Expression and Validating Responses: A Transactional Model for Understanding Individual and Relationship Distress." In *Support Processes in Intimate Relationships,* ed. K. T. Sullivan and J. Davila, 121–50. New York: Oxford University Press.

Gray, A. W., B. Parkinson, and R. I. Dunbar. 2015. "Laughter's Influence on the Intimacy of Self-Disclosure." *Human Nature* 26: 28–43. doi.org/10.1007/s12110-015-9225-8.

Gutierrez, E. 2013. "A Rat in the Labyrinth of Anorexia Nervosa: Contributions of the Activity-Based Anorexia Rodent Model to the Understanding of Anorexia Nervosa." *The International Journal of Eating Disorders* 46, no. 4: 289–301. doi.org/10.1002/eat.22095.

Hall, J. A. 2012. "Friendship Standards: The Dimensions of Ideal Expectations." *Journal of Social and Personal Relationships* 29, no. 7: 884–907. doi:10.1177/0265407512448274.

————. 2018. "How Many Hours Does It Take to Make a Friend?" *Journal of Social and Personal Relationships* 36, no. 4: 1278–96. doi.org/10.1177/0265407518761225.

Kashy, D. A., and B. M. DePaulo. 1996. "Who Lies?" *Journal of Personality and Social Psychology* 70, no. 5: 1037–51. doi:10.1037/0022-3514.70.5.1037.

Kross, E., M. G. Berman, W. Mischel, E. E. Smith, and T. D. Wager. 2011. "Social Rejection Shares Somatosensory Representations with Physical Pain." *Proceedings of the National Academy of Sciences* 108, no. 15: 6270–75. doi:10.1073/pnas.1102693108.

Kurtz, L. E., and S. B. Algoe. 2015. "Putting Laughter in Context: Shared Laughter as Behavioral Indicator of Relationship Well-Being. *Personal Relationships* 22, no. 4: 573–90. doi.org/10.1111/pere.12095.

Lenz, A. S., P. James, C. Stewart, M. Simic, R. Hempel, and S. Carr. 2021. "A Preliminary Validation of the Youth Over- and Under-Control (YOU-C) Screening Measure with a Community Sample." *International Journal for the Advancement of Counselling.* doi.org/10.1007/s10447-021-09439-9.

Linehan, M. M. 1997. Validation and psychotherapy. In *Empathy Reconsidered: New Directions in Psychotherapy*, ed. A. Bohart and L. Greenberg, 353–392. Washington, DC: American Psychological Assocation.

Lynch, T. 2018a. *Radically Open Dialectical Behavior Therapy: Theory and Practice for Treating Disorders of Overcontrol.* Oakland, CA: New Harbinger.

————. 2018b. *The Skills Training Manual for Radically Open Dialectical Behavior Therapy: A Clinician's Guide for Treating Disorders of Overcontrol.* Oakland, CA: New Harbinger.

Marche, K., A.-C. Martel, and P. Apicella. 2017. "Differences between Dorsal and Ventral Striatum in the Sensitivity of Tonically Active Neurons to Rewarding Events." *Frontiers in Systems Neuroscience* 11: 52. doi.org/10.3389/fnsys.2017.00052.

Markway, B., and C. Ampel. 2018. *The Self-Confidence Workbook: A Guide to Overcoming Self-Doubt and Improving Self-Esteem.* San Antonio, TX: Althea Press.

McEvoy, P. M., Nathan, P., & Norton, P. J. 2009. "Efficacy of transdiagnostic treatments: A review of published outcome studies and future research directions." *Journal of Cognitive Psychotherapy* 23, no. 1: 20–33. https://doi.org/10.1891/0889-8391.23.1.20

Miles, L., and L. Johnston. 2007. Detecting happiness: Perceiver sensitivity to enjoyment and non-enjoyment smiles. *Journal of Nonverbal Behavior*, 31: 259–275.

Savitsky, K., B. Keysar, N. Epley, T. Carter, and A. Swanson. 2011. "The Closeness Communication Bias: Increased Egocentrism Among Friends Versus Strangers." *Journal of Experimental Social Psychology* 47, no. 1: 269–73.

Sergerie, K., C. Chochol, and J. L. Armony. 2008. "The Role of the Amygdala in Emotional Processing: A Quantitative Meta-Analysis of Functional Neuroimaging Studies." *Neuroscience and Biobehavioral Reviews* 32, no. 4: 811–30. doi.org/10.1016/j.neubiorev.2007.12.002.

Small, M. L. 2017. *Someone to Talk To: How Networks Matter in Practice.* New York: Oxford University Press.

Smither, J. W., M. London, and R. R. Reilly. 2005. "Does Performance Improve Following Multisource Feedback? A Theoretical Model, Meta-Analysis, and Review of Empirical Findings." *Personnel Psychology* 58, no. 1: 33–66. doi.org/10.1111/j.1744-6570.2005.514_1.x.

Song, R., H. Over, and M. Carpenter. 2016. "Young Children Discriminate Genuine from Fake Smiles and Expect People Displaying Genuine Smiles to Be More Prosocial." *Evolution and Human Behavior* 37, no. 6: 490–501.

Vansteenwegen, D., C. Iberico, B. Vervliet, V. Marescau, and D. Hermans. 2008. "Contextual Fear Induced by Unpredictability in a Human Fear Conditioning Preparation Is Related to the Chronic Expectation of a Threatening US." *Biological Psychology* 77, no. 1: 39–46. doi.org/10.1016/j.biopsycho.2007.08.012.

Karyn D. Hall, PhD, is founder and director of Dialectical Behavior Therapies Center in Houston, TX. She is a radically open dialectical behavior therapy (RO DBT) supervisor, and is a certified Linehan DBT Board of Certification clinician. Hall provides both individual and team supervision in RO DBT and DBT. She specializes in the treatment of individuals with maladaptive overcontrolled coping.

Ellen Astrachan-Fletcher, PhD, FAED, CEDS-S, is midwest regional clinical director at Eating Recovery Center and Pathlight Mood and Anxiety Center. She is a lecturer at the Feinberg School of Medicine, Northwestern University, and associate professor of psychiatry at UIC. She has more than thirty years of clinical and teaching experience in the field. She is a nationally recognized expert in the field of eating disorders. She coauthored *The Dialectical Behavior Therapy Skills Workbook for Bulimia*, which is used at eating disorders treatment facilities throughout the country.

Mima Simic, MD, is a consultant child and adolescent psychiatrist, and joint head of the Maudsley Centre for Child and Adolescent Eating Disorders (MCCAED) in London, UK. She was consultant to the adolescent DBT team, and led development of the intensive day treatment program (ITP) at the Maudsley Hospital. Simic is an internationally recognized expert in the field of child and adolescent eating disorders. She is senior RO DBT clinician, senior trainer, and supervisor for the Maudsley family and multi-family therapy for eating disorders.

Foreword writer **Thomas R. Lynch, PhD, FBPsS**, is founder of RO DBT; and author of the seminal text, *Radically Open Dialectical Behavior Therapy*.

FROM OUR COFOUNDER—

As cofounder of New Harbinger and a clinical psychologist since 1978, I know that emotional problems are best helped with evidence-based therapies. These are the treatments derived from scientific research (randomized controlled trials) that show what works. Whether these treatments are delivered by trained clinicians or found in a self-help book, they are designed to provide you with proven strategies to overcome your problem.

Therapies that aren't evidence-based—whether offered by clinicians or in books—are much less likely to help. In fact, therapies that aren't guided by science may not help you at all. That's why this New Harbinger book is based on scientific evidence that the treatment can relieve emotional pain.

This is important: if this book isn't enough, and you need the help of a skilled therapist, use the following resources to find a clinician trained in the evidence-based protocols appropriate for your problem. And if you need more support—a community that understands what you're going through and can show you ways to cope—resources for that are provided below, as well.

Real help is available for the problems you have been struggling with. The skills you can learn from evidence-based therapies will change your life.

Matthew McKay, PhD
Cofounder, New Harbinger Publications

MORE BOOKS from
NEW HARBINGER PUBLICATIONS

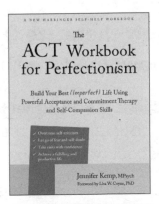

POCKET THERAPY FOR EMOTIONAL BALANCE

Quick DBT Skills to Manage Intense Emotions

978-1684037674 / US $14.95

THE ACT WORKBOOK FOR PERFECTIONISM

Build Your Best (Imperfect) Life Using Powerful Acceptance and Commitment Therapy and Self-Compassion Skills

978-1684038077 / US $24.95

DON'T LET YOUR EMOTIONS RUN YOUR LIFE

How Dialectical Behavior Therapy Can Put You in Control

978-1572243095 / US $20.95

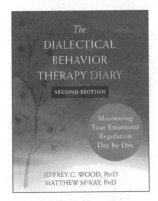

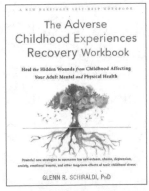

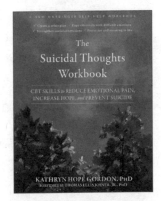

THE DIALECTICAL BEHAVIOR THERAPY DIARY, SECOND EDITION

Monitoring Your Emotional Regulation Day by Day

978-1684037735 / US $16.95

THE ADVERSE CHILDHOOD EXPERIENCES RECOVERY WORKBOOK

Heal the Hidden Wounds from Childhood Affecting Your Adult Mental and Physical Health

978-1684036646 / US $24.95

THE SUICIDAL THOUGHTS WORKBOOK

CBT Skills to Reduce Emotional Pain, Increase Hope, and Prevent Suicide

978-1684037025 / US $21.95

🌱 **newharbinger**publications

1-800-748-6273 / newharbinger.com

(VISA, MC, AMEX / prices subject to change without notice)
Follow Us 📷 f 🐦 ▶ 📌 in

Did you know there are **free tools** you can download for this book?

Free tools are things like **worksheets**, **guided meditation exercises**, and **more** that will help you get the most out of your book.

You can download free tools for this book—whether you bought or borrowed it, in any format, from any source—from the New Harbinger website. All you need is a NewHarbinger.com account. Just use the URL provided in this book to view the free tools that are available for it. Then, click on the "download" button for the free tool you want, and follow the prompts that appear to log in to your NewHarbinger.com account and download the material.

You can also save the free tools for this book to your **Free Tools Library** so you can access them again anytime, just by logging in to your account! Just look for this button on the book's free tools page.

+ Save this to my free tools library

If you need help accessing or downloading free tools, visit **newharbinger.com/faq** or contact us at **customerservice@newharbinger.com**.